20/20 Vision

Select Poems and Stories from the 33rd Annual National Capital Writing Contest

Published by Canadian Authors Association–National Capital Region
Designed by Crowe Creations
Edited by Sherrill Wark

Canadian Authors Association–National Capital Region
https://canadianauthors.org/nationalcapitalregion/

First Canadian Authors Association–National Capital Region Edition
April 2020

Cover photo from iStock. Credit: Ruslan Dashinsky. ID: 1130253931
Text and Headings set in Gothic720 Lt BT

Cover design © 2020 by Crowe Creations
Interior design © 2020 by Crowe Creations

crowecreations.ca

Canadian Authors Association–National Capital Region
ISBN: 978-0-9869031-2-0

To the artistic soul in each of us.

"Writing is no trouble: you just jot down ideas as
they occur to you. The jotting is
simplicity itself — it is the
occurring which is difficult."

Stephen Leacock

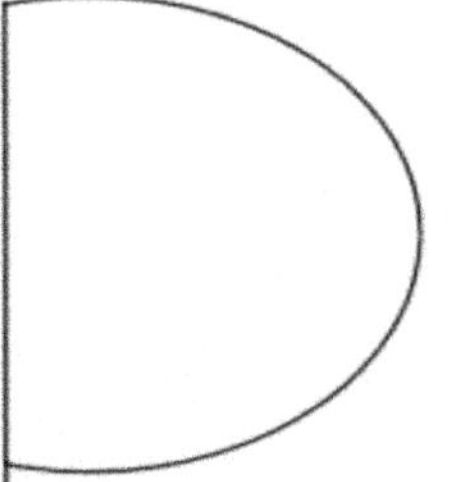

PRESIDENT'S MESSAGE

My favourite thing about the National Capital Writing Contest (NCWC) is that we never know what to expect.

The poetry and short story categories are open to any genre and style, and that leaves the imaginations of our writers unfettered. The results never fail to surprise, pique curiosity, or make readers look at a situation in a new way. And so it was for the 2020 contest.

The year 2020 … those numbers sparked an idea in the brain of the coordinator of the contest, Sherrill Wark. "Let's do an anthology this year," she said. "We could call it *20/20 Vision*."

Brilliant, right?

Those with 20/20 vision see clearly so they can navigate what's ahead of them without faltering. The poems and stories in this anthology are the way forward for the authors. They are building blocks for future success.

I also associate 20/20 vision with hindsight, the ability to learn from the past. The writers of these poems and stories have been honing their craft, learning from others, and learning from mistakes.

A 20/20 anthology is also fitting for the Canadian Authors Association (CAA) because we are on the eve of 100th anniversary.

In 1921, a group of prominent Canadian authors, including Stephen Leacock, banded together to lobby for authors' rights. Over the one-hundred-year history of CAA, many things have changed and many stayed the same.

This book you hold in your hand is a perfect example. We published this book. We did it without a big-name publishing house because technology has provided publication alternatives. That same technology means that it is easier to copy and distribute writers' work without authorization, so protecting intellectual property is an ongoing challenge.

That tension between forward and back, release and protect is the tightrope-walk of every writer. We sponsor this contest to support and encourage professional and emerging writers and to release their work in a way that honours and protects their rights as writers.

I want to congratulate this year's finalists. We are proud to showcase their work here.

And I want to thank Sherrill Wark for managing thousands of details, juggling all the entries, and creating such a beautiful product.

Arlene Smith
President, CAA-NCR

ARLENE SMITH

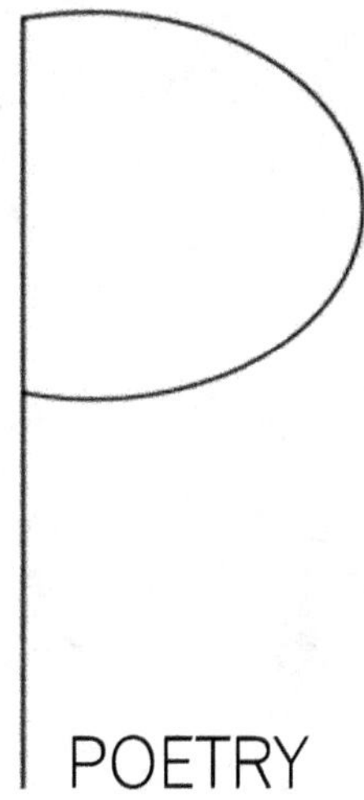

POETRY

GILL FOSS

POETRY JUDGE

As a member of the local branch of Canadian Authors Association (CAA), Gill Foss was actively immersed in the local Arts scene during her thirty-four years in Nepean before moving to a more-rural property in the Ottawa Valley. She is on the executive of the National Capital Region (Ottawa/Gatineau) as the Branch Historian. Several years ago she Chaired the prestigious CAA National Literary Awards program (poetry) for four years before taking over as National President. She also belongs to Haiku Canada, The Ontario Poetry Society and continues as a member of the Ottawa Field Stone Poets who hold regular discussion/criticism sessions each month.

Over the years, Ms Foss has participated in national conferences, attended seminars and writing courses to hone her appreciation of the current approaches to poetic forms/perceptions, during which times she has met many interesting and influential members in the field of modern poetry.

Gill Foss has consistently entered* contests and continues to contribute to many anthologies. She has two chapbooks published (lyric, 2008; haiku, 2011). Her new book collection, *Personal Perspectives*, appeared late 2019. She continues to attend local events whenever possible.

*And placed in.

FIRST PLACE, POETRY

JOAN McKAY

"THIS INVENTED WORLD"

Joan McKay says poetry is her first love. She believes that every creative act, no matter the medium, has the potential to change our world. She has been a frequent winner in the Canadian Authors' Association annual NCWC contest, a finalist in Malahat's Long Poem contest, and won the Irish Comórtais Liteartha for poetry in Irish in the Diaspora. Joan lives in Kingston, Ontario, where she enjoys taking yoga classes and studying Irish Gaelic and Italian.

"this invented world"

> ... the cloud preceded us
> There was a muddy centre before we breathed.
> There was a myth before the myth began,
> Venerable and articulate and complete.
> Wallace Stevens, *Toward a Supreme Fiction*

Image preceded word.
Etched in deepest brain,
inscribed there in time
before remembered time,
it is elusive, an image which only hints
at truths too precious
to lose in shifting ancient mist,
so fleeting we fear they might be beautiful lies,
not understanding as we struggle thus,
... the cloud preceded us.

The gentle closing of the fontanel
sealed the door to other worlds,
to time when knowing how we began,
with a clarity we'd seldom feel again,
was gone — our first life loss,
a separation we have grieved
forever, the not-quite-us-ness of our wanderings
amidst valleys of absent memory
suggesting that, in all we've achieved,
there was a muddy centre before we breathed.

What is this constant search for why,
or how, the rhyme or rune
which ghosts our path?
What soul-companion beckons us to destiny
or death, rejects our claims of innocence,
demands, as compensation for the shortest span
on earth, a propitiation to Olympian gods
who whisper from eons before our birth:
there was a plan,
there was a myth before the myth began.

And now, this moment, grounded in word and metaphor,
in a learned arrangement of symbols,
the search for clarity remains elusive,
heart song still tugs at the edges of recall,
images slip endlessly from our grasp,
our brushes with past life remain heartbreakingly fleet.
We cling to the thought of one eye to see and one to feel,
and question if we need such twinning to find our way,
such balance to make us feel replete,
venerable and articulate and complete.

Judge's Comment

In this Glosa, based on four lines from Wallace Stephens's *Toward a Supreme Fiction*, the poet follows Stephens's philosophical belief in lyrical meditation and the interaction of reality with imagination. The form he/she chose perfectly illustrates the illusiveness of life in the image of "shifting ancient mist" and "muddy centre" before existence was reined in by words. The requirement of rhyme for the sixth, ninth and tenth lines in each stanza is followed with skill to prolong each thought with no unwarranted impact. The piece flows seamlessly as each ten-line verse builds on the one before to culminate in a poem that proves imagination is the foundation of good lyric poetry. Congratulations!

SECOND PLACE, POETRY

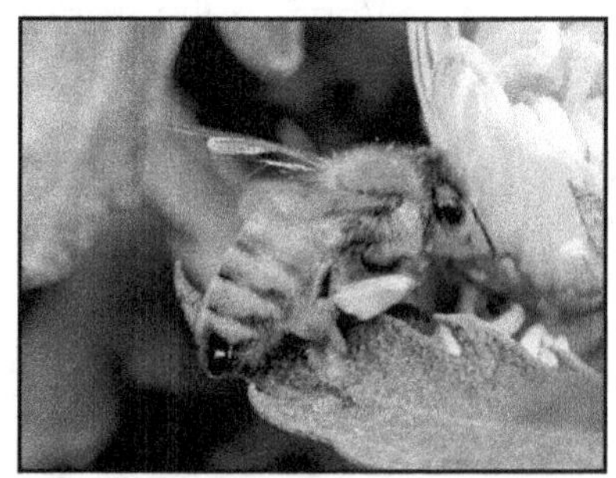

MILLER ADAMS

PANTOUM FOR THE HONEY BEE

Pantoum for the Honey Bee

When the bees are gone, we'll all be gone.
How could we live without honey combs?
The earth will be barren, history 's blinds drawn,
and hives only hushed and abandoned homes.

What would we do without honey combs?
The grumbling old queen will abdicate,
when the hives are all hushed and abandoned homes
and doddering workers can' t carry their freight.

The grumbling old queen will abdicate,
the drones, crumbled ashes, their work long done;
doddering workers relinquish their freight,
while blossoms are withering under the sun.

The drones are just ash, their work long done.
Their bodies will lie where their bodies have fallen.
All the blossoms will wither under the sun
with nothing to pluck and carry their pollen.

Our bodies will lie where our bodies have fallen.
No one will give thanks for their daily bread
with nothing to pluck and carry the pollen
and no table replete with a banquet's spread;

no queen in the parlour eating honey and bread;
the counting-house kingless, still as a tomb;
no table laid out with a banquet's spread,
no sherry and port in the drawing room.

The counting-house kingless, still as a tomb,
no guests at a soiree, no knock on the door,
no sherry and port in the drawing room,
a moneyless bank, an abandoned store.

No guests at a soiree, no knock on the door;
classrooms without children, no one to teach,
a moneyless bank, an abandoned store,
a cottage unthatched, a deserted beach,

a class without children, a bank without money;
inventions, hostilities, triumphs unlisted;
hives without bees, dry bread without honey —
no one to remember we ever existed.

Miller Adams is the author of *Instructions for Lies and Flowers* and the forthcoming poetry collection, *Folding Laundry on Judgment Day*. Previously writing as Sylvia Adams, she published a novel, two poetry collections, and a children's book. A writing instructor, book reviewer, and founding member of Ottawa's Field Stone Poets, she is the winner of several awards, including the Diana Brebner prize and two Aesthetica poetry competitions.

Judge's Comment

The poet of this piece has chosen a difficult format as the basis for a poem dealing with a very important topic of the day — the continued sustainability of our global food supply — and has accomplished this both with skill and extended relevant nursery-rhyme humour. The repetition demanded by the form only emphasizes the importance of the subject. Each inhabitant of the hive is recognized for its importance in the production of the final product. I give kudos to a poet who can use poetry effectively to draw much-needed attention to a global threat in such a thought-provoking way. Well done.

Judge's Comment

I really enjoyed the imaginative opening conceit of an artist creating the morning with her brush. The addition of the monarch butterfly "stuttering along the beach" in its "erratic flight", the kayak "windmilling" across the water, the shades of green and smoky blue all fill out the enchanting idea. Throughout, the imagery holds surprises like telescopic cameras that "caterpillar" toward the woods and a picnic table that "welcomes" friends to "unwrap their lives" "next to coffee and muffins". To close the story, our artist/poet considers the later season colours, ending with the grey, migrating geese. Finally, a most lively depiction of a riverside throughout the year and an example of an unusual turn of imagery that really works well. PS. I had to look in the dictionary for the meaning of "Riparian"!

THIRD PLACE, POETRY

Summer on the Riparian Corridor

Morning arrives at the bay
wearing cotton and a wide-brimmed hat.
She perches on the rocky, layered beach,
considers colours for rocks and trees,
washes sunshine across the day,
paints a gentle breeze on water and wispy,
cotton-candy clouds overhead. Slowly
the day emerges from her brush tip.

A monarch butterfly stutters along the beach,
orange-and-black wings fanning figure-eights.
It warms itself on a rock, resumes
an erratic flight in search of milkweed.

A kayak windmills across the water, sunlight
glinting on wet blades: left, right, left. It glides
past haunts of soaring eagles,
an alcove of grazing deer,
shallow waters of sunning turtles. And
in the distance, white triangles billow
against the horizon, its hills in shades of green
and smoky blue.

At the edge of the water, a sharp knife slides
between white flesh and scaly skin, a glistening
filet — the catch of the day.

Telescopic cameras caterpillar through
the parking lot to the woods in search of rare birds,
and in the distance, the pop-a-pop-pop
from the rifle range, and its echoing
pop-a-pop-pop.

GERRY MOONEY

Nepean poet, Gerry Mooney, is a member of The Ontario Poetry Society (TOPS) and a recent addition to Ottawa's Field Stone Poets. Her work has won awards and appeared in a number of Canadian anthologies and on-line. Her favourite topic is anything to do with nature. Other than poetry, she enjoys music, golfing, Nordic walking and working out in the gym.

SUMMER ON THE RIPARIAN CORRIDOR

Sun worshippers lather lotion on winter-white
skin, turn slowly like meat on a spit waiting
for tones of gold and bronze, doze
to the drone of cicadas.

A shaded picnic table welcomes friends
and for a few hours they laugh and unwrap
their lives setting them on the table
next to coffee and muffins. Leaving,
they lament the passing of time, promise
to meet again sooner.

And on the beach, the lady in the wide-brimmed hat
will soon pull a sweater over her shoulders, consider
yellows and reds for the hills, browns and
greys for vees of migrating geese.

HONOURABLE MENTION

BEV CHAMBERS

DANCE CLASS

Bev Chambers started writing poetry four years ago following the loss of her family's beloved golden retriever. She was further inspired by her family and members of her writing group. Her poetry has been published in The National Capital Writing Contest's 30th Anniversary Anthology, 2017 (honourable mention), and *Canadian Stories*. Bev also writes creative non-fiction short stories, which have been published in a variety of media. She lives with her husband and his radio collection in Kingston.

Dance Class

We meet upstairs in our allotted space,
Hands pushing walkers, holding canes,
which we now put aside.

Our hands extend in friendship
as we greet one another,
And sit down in readiness for our class.

Our teacher's smooth hands guide us,
Her words soft and warm,
Wrapping around us with encouragement.

Our fingers flutter to the strains of the cello,
Hands tap to the beat of the drum,
Now opening with possibilities,
Now closing with purpose.

Strong hands that have worked decades
Shaping the community,
Beautiful in their determination.

Standing now we hold each other's hands,
In the circle
we move differently yet as one,
Whole in our togetherness.

We raise our clasped hands to the ceiling,
Petals unfurling towards the sun.
Graceful hands,
tremoring with the burden of this disease.

Judge's Comment

This poem appears to be about those with a disability and how they work through its challenges. It addresses the symptoms with sympathy, understanding and a resolve not to give up against mounting frailty. Putting aside sticks and walkers, the little group joins hands for "togetherness", following the directions of the teacher as they move to the rhythms of drum and cello, to end by unfurling hands gracefully "tremoring with the burden of this disease". An uplifting take on acceptance and determination. Thank you for your inspiring approach.

HONOURABLE MENTION

PAT MCLAUGHLIN

MY WORD

Pat McLaughlin

has been writing poetry since January 2018. It all started with an online poetry workshop, and blossomed into a collection of poems on Aging. An avid painter, she kept a travel journal during a three-year travel spree as a Meanderthal, joined a couple of writing groups, took more poetry courses and continues to look for ways to expand her horizons. Playing with words and writing poetry gives her air to breathe!

Judge's Comment

This poem, written long and thin — although not in concrete form — carries a punch that outweighs its size. A semi-humorous take on the odd "senior moment" that bugs us all as we have to admit to occasional "word slippage" as the poet "stalks a synonym" until later "the traitor appears". It ends philosophically with the admission of "Alas!" that "old hood" isn't good.

My Word

Lost my word
How absurd
It was just there
under my hair
Now it's gone
Damnation
Tongue to brain
must regain
word power
this hour
Can't talk
Must stalk
a synonym
Feeling dim
Mind is blank
dark and dank

Sometime later
the traitor
appears
and jeers
Time has past
Feeling cast
into *old hood*
which isn't good

Alas!

HONOURABLE MENTION

ADRIENNE STEVENSON

POLITICAL PANTOUM

Adrienne Stevenson

has lived in Ottawa since 1974. A retired forensic scientist, she writes poetry, fiction and creative non-fiction. Her poetry has been published in *Quills*, *Scarlet Leaf Review*, *Blood & Bourbon*, *The Wire's Dream*, Ottawa Poets Pathway "*Lampman Challenge*" chapbook, "*Time and Again Poetry Anthology*" chapbook. Her stories have won prizes in contests held by Capital Crime Writers, Canadian Authors Association and the Ottawa Public Library, and some have been published in *Byline.*

Judge's Comment

Once again, a poet has used the strict form of the pantoum to underscore our continued antipathy toward the "political disease" that is fuelling hatred and fear across the world. After each bout, the world insists "never again", but with each new election, the two insanities return with a vengeance. It is a sad and angry poem again making use of the repetition of lines to draw attention to the futility of repeated insanity. Well stated with impact.

Political Pantoum

Flags wave in the summer breeze
heat enters the human brain
fear and hate spread like disease
people become vicious, insane

Heat enters the human brain
haven't we been here before?
people become vicious, insane
no one remembers the recent war

Haven't we been here before?
didn't we quell the monstrous urge?
no one remembers the recent war
those who suffered the latest purge

Didn't we quell the monstrous urge?
everyone thought those days were done
those who suffered the latest purge
hoped against hope this had not begun

Everyone thought those days were done
they lined up again to cast their vote
hoped against hope this had not begun
fresh agony knells a discordant note

They lined up again to cast their vote
flags wave in the summer breeze
fresh agony knells a discordant note
fear and hate spread like disease

Susan J. Atkinson's poems have won a number of awards, including first prize in the National Capital Writers Contest in 2019. Her poems have appeared in such journals as *The Antigonish Review*, *Arc Magazine*, *The Dalhousie Review*, *Bywords*, *The New Quarterly*, *Room*, and *ottawater*. She is currently working on her first full-length collection and a new chapbook.

FINALIST

SUSAN J. ATKINSON

SOMETHING BEAUTIFUL

Something Beautiful

On a cold November afternoon my class of six-year olds
and I read the picture book *Something Beautiful.* We cry

for the elderly lady who lives on an alley-way doorstep
in a cardboard box. She is wrapped in a thick plastic

cape for warmth and in the background of the picture
shattered glass from a bottle sparkles like *fallen stars.*

On scraps of paper the children design a new home —
their something beautiful for the old lady in the cardboard box.

Most draw castles and palaces with hearts and flowers
blooming from colourful walls, except my new student

uprooted from Syria and coarsely planted in this new country.
On his square of white-paper he draws what he knows about home.

A fighter jet shrieks through a grey sky darkened still from the
pressure of his stubby pencil pinned in one spot.

Bombs drop on a row of roofs destroying all the houses but one.
My boy colours fiery smoke wrapping around his memory.

Out of his paler grey wisps a kaleidoscope of butterflies
burst and flutter above the destruction —

his something beautiful shaded mauve and blue
yellow hearts shining on each perfectly curved wing.

Something Beautiful, written by Sharon Dennis Wyeth

Judge's Comment

I like the way this simple classroom project shows how much the understanding of a refugee's experience needs to be appreciated in a North American setting. This simple story, told in couplets, shows the differing appreciation of beauty and safety when seen through the experience of a war-torn childhood when beauty means butterflies and hearts, not palaces.

FINALIST

PAULINE IRVING

ACROSTIC ON AGING

Pauline Irving was born in Halifax, Nova Scotia, as Pauline Flinn. In her twenties, she relocated to Ottawa and attended Carleton University. She worked for the Federal Government for twenty-six years. She currently works with her husband in their golf business. She enrolled in a "Writing for Enjoyment" class in Kanata in 1999 and continues taking classes and writing as a hobby.

Judge's Comment

This poem is created using an alphabet of reasons illustrating why getting older is not to be seen as a travesty based solely on accumulating numbers. It encapsulates one of the main themes addressed by the poets in this year's contest. It starts by asking why getting older is the wrong thing to do and ends by cautioning us that we will all be "one of those seniors" one day. Each point raised is well worth consideration.

Acrostic on Aging

A Aging is a part of life for everyone
B But when did it get to be the wrong thing to do
C Counting the years is something everyone goes through
D Definitely a time where youth is revered
E Every added-on year somehow is seen as a liability
F Forever young is not possible, don't they realize
G Getting older is not a total disgrace
H Having those years of experience is an advantage
I If only the younger ones would realize this
J Just being young is a fleeting claim to fame
K Keeping sharp mind, body and soul are admirable
L Loving each stage of life is important
M Mirrors show wisdom and learning not just wrinkles
N Not being young is far from a crime
O Oh to be valued whatever your age
P Prejudice because of age is as bad as all prejudices
Q Quite despicable to be mistreated because of a number
R Respect and appreciation are warranted by all
S Superiority is not automatically granted to youth
T Time and a life well-lived are to be admired
U Unnecessary disregard for seniors is a travesty
V Value the person and do not focus on the number
W Wisdom is part of the aging process
X Xclude not the value of the person who has aged
Y You will be one of those seniors one day
Z Zealous and vital can apply to any age.

FINALIST

ADRIENNE STEVENSON

HOMOPHONY, HOMOPHOBY

Adrienne Stevenson has lived in Ottawa since 1974. A retired forensic scientist, she writes poetry, fiction and creative non-fiction. Her poetry has been published in *Quills*, *Scarlet Leaf Review*, *Blood & Bourbon*, *The Wire's Dream*, Ottawa Poets Pathway "*Lampman Challenge*" chapbook, "*Time and Again Poetry Anthology*" chapbook. Her stories have won prizes in contests held by Capital Crime Writers, Canadian Authors Association, and the Ottawa Public Library, and some have been published in the CAA National Capital Region's newsletter, *Byline.*

Judge's Comment

I like the clever juxtaposition of the two words in each line that have the same sound when read aloud but mean very different things from the listener's point of view. Throughout the poem, these words build on each other to bring the woman from a subservient life of intimidation to overcome imposed obstacles and reach her potential in the world as a writer. A triumph based on the astute build-up of words.

Homophony, Homophoby

the woman at the kitchen sink is out of sync
a mirrored pane reflects her pain
she prays that she not become prey
to the madman of the week, who thinks her weak
she will stare him down from her stair-top
and send him down the road he rode in on

the world chews over her right to choose
but the nit-picking flea does not cause her to flee
she may groan over delays, but her rights have grown
the lengthy wait always a weight on her thoughts

she has striven for the right to write
now allowed to speak her thoughts aloud
the band plays what was formerly banned
the sealing on the glass ceiling erodes
someday the world will not be zero-sum

FINALIST

ADRIENNE STEVENSON

NELSON NZ HARBOUR VIEWS, 2019

Adrienne Stevenson has lived in Ottawa since 1974. A retired forensic scientist, she writes poetry, fiction and creative non-fiction. Her poetry has been published in *Quills*, *Scarlet Leaf Review*, *Blood & Bourbon*, *The Wire's Dream*, Ottawa Poets Pathway "*Lampman Challenge*" chapbook, "*Time and Again Poetry Anthology*" chapbook. Her stories have won prizes in contests held by Capital Crime Writers, Canadian Authors Association, and the Ottawa Public Library, and some have been published in the CAA National Capital Region's newsletter, *Byline*.

Nelson NZ Harbour Views, 2019

Out where the boulder bank restrains the sea
sailboats of many classes ebb and flow
vivid boat-butterflies in a bobbing row,
spinnakers swelling as they pass the quay,
head through the cut to deeps where they are free
to race, and set their sheets to catch the blow
that sweeps some to success; leaves others slow
but not at all discouraged in esprit.

Back on land, the wind bears no goodwill;
it fans the flame set by a tiny spark
our view now smoke-filled, fiery nighttime glow
obscures the stars and ravages distant hills,
chokes both land and livestock, closes parks,
six weeks will pass before its overthrow.

Judge's Comment

I enjoy poems that dwell on topics of great events and I can't think of any more important than the recent horrendous fires in Australia. The poet here has used the change of pace between the first eight and final six lines to delineate the opposing views of the devastating effect of wind to stark effect. A very relevant piece of work. Well done.

SHORT
STORIES

CHRISTINE McNAIR

SHORT STORY JUDGE

Christine McNair is the author of *Charm* (Book*hug, 2017) and *Conflict* (Book*hug, 2012). *Charm* won the Archibald Lampman Award in 2018 and *Conflict* was a finalist for the City of Ottawa Book Award, the Archibald Lampman Award, and the ReLit Award, as well as being previously shortlisted for the Robert Kroetsch Award for Innovative Poetry. Her chapbook *pleasantries and other misdemeanours* (2013; Apt9 press) was shortlisted for the bpNichol chapbook award. She won second prize (poetry) in the Writers' Federation of Nova Scotia writing contest and an honourable mention in the Eden Mills Literary competition.

Her work has appeared in *Arc Poetry Magazine, CV2, Descant, Poetry is Dead, Prairie Fire*, and sundry other places. In her past life, she worked as an editor's devil (editorial assistant) at Gaspereau Press and was the co-publisher of Chaudiere Books. She is currently working on her third book, a hybrid literary non-fiction and poetry manuscript focusing on preeclampsia. McNair currently lives in Ottawa, where she works as a book doctor.

FIRST PLACE, SHORT STORY

THERESA ANN WALLACE

WATER, FIRE, AIR

Bradley's mother leaned on the kitchen counter.

"Just go," she said. "You know. Do the things you used to." The sleeves of her robe dangled into last night's dinner dishes. She sucked her cigarette, squinted against the smoke drifting up to her pink sponge curlers. "Two months is long enough."

His father was waiting for him by the stairs. He beckoned Bradley like a cop impatient to keep traffic flowing. "Your mother's right." He pointed at the door. "We're all in the army, son. Not just me."

Bradley shoved his hands into the pockets of his parka and plodded up the street. He kept his eyes on the sidewalk, avoiding the gaze of the paperboy tossing newspapers onto front stoops. The wind gnawed through his jeans. His thighs ached, then went numb with cold.

He turned onto the main street of the army base and paused at the entrance to the rec centre, filling his lungs.

The soles of his boots squeaked on the

shiny linoleum in the lobby. As he passed the bowling alley, a ball thumped against hardwood and rolled down a lane. He winced at the shudder in his chest when the pins clattered and fell. Girls shrieked. They were probably having a birthday party. Other families still celebrated birthdays. He'd be thirteen in two weeks, which meant nothing to anybody now. In that other life, he won competitions in archery and gymnastics. He learned how to tie military knots and how to climb up the fishnet ropes on the gym wall. His instructors had called him Monkey.

He pulled his ID card out of his back pocket and slid it face down across the counter. A young private picked it up. He whispered with another attendant, their heads together, then they turned in unison to Bradley, their smiles pasted on. The private relieved a lock and key from a hook and hung up Bradley's card.

On the pool deck, two girls in droopy pink bathing suits giggled and darted by. They looked about his sister's age. He headed for the deep end. His toes pierced the water and he sank with a muted splash, down, down, down to the bottom, alternately sculling his hands then pushing the water, palms up, over his head to prevent his body from bobbing to the surface.

Far above him, swimmers stroked in slow motion. He fought against the urge to kick, willed himself to take a breath in through his nose and mouth, to flood his lungs, to stay under. He squeezed his eyes shut. Saw blackness, a chalkboard wiped clean. Suddenly, he kicked hard and torpedoed into the light, sputtering and heaving.

The lifeguard approached. "You okay?"

"Yeah." he said. Casual. Cool. "Fine." He coughed, rolling as nonchalantly as he could onto the slippery deck. He gave the lifeguard a little wave as he stood, trying to control the shaking in his legs.

***

I know when I open the door that I'm not supposed to. But I do it anyway. I'm curious, and a bit lonely. Bored too, babysitting my sister. My parents have gone to a New Year's Eve party at the officers' mess and my older brother is out with his friends. Everyone having fun but me. I've just finished playing *Snakes and Ladders* with Suzie. I hate *Snakes and Ladders* because it's so random. I've bribed her with lots of money to play *Monopoly*, and so far, she hasn't kicked the pieces off the board.

We're stretched out on the living room floor when the doorbell rings. "We're not supposed to answer that, Bradley." Suzie rests her chin on her fists and doesn't look up. For a five-year-old, she's such a know-it-all.

"What if it's an emergency?"

Nobody uses our front door, but somebody's pounding on it. The door is only ten steps away, so it's not like I have a lot of time to think about whether what I'm doing is right or wrong.

"Hey, that's cold." Suzie sounds miffed. A sweep of wind ruffles her play money.

Robbie from next door shivers on the front steps. He's not wearing a jacket. A plug of grey snot blocks each nostril and the tips of his ears are pink. "Got a new hockey game for Christmas. Want to come over?" Robbie grins, hopeful.

I hesitate. Even though he's a year younger than me, Robbie and I play together sometimes, but I'm not allowed inside his place. He's one of ten kids and my parents say there's always a kerfuffle going on at his place. They're right. Robbie's mother, her ratty slippers sliding on the snow, once chased his sister down the street. His mother was waving a broom over her head and swearing. His sister's nightgown flowed behind her and she ran without looking back, like she knew what would happen if she was caught.

"I'm babysitting Suzie," I tell Robbie.

"She can come." He shows me his palms like he's begging.

He really wants me to see his new table hockey game. I asked for one for Christmas but my mother just shrugged and said maybe next year.

"Okay," I say finally. "But we can't stay long."

***

"Make that with brown sugar, Bradley. It's healthier."

He'd already buttered the Wonder bread and was shaking a spoonful of white sugar onto each slice. He ignored her, slapped the pieces together and tore a hunk of sandwich with his teeth.

His mother was cleaning, waxing and buffing the kitchen floor until it shone like the buttons on his dad's dress uniform. Next week she'd announce the floor looked yellow; she'd get down on her hands and knees and scrape it with a paring knife. Then she'd wax and polish it again.

"When you're done, I need you to go to Safeway." She steered the floor polisher around his feet, staring at them pointedly to tell him he was in the way.

He didn't know why, but his parents hadn't forced him to go to the pool again. Instead, every day this week his mother had put change in his hand, then shooed him up the lane to the grocery store. He tramped across the empty field to the road, along dirty snowbanks — it hadn't snowed much that winter — and over to the shopping plaza. A ten-minute walk at most, but she must have wanted to be rid of him. They didn't run out of milk every day by accident.

He bought the carton of milk and snuck around back of the plaza, fingering the pack of matches he'd swiped off the kitchen counter. Where the pavement ended, he slipped into the woods on a narrow path nobody would notice unless they knew about it. Along the way, he picked up empty cigarette packages, a grease-stained paper bag, anything that looked like it would burn. The path stopped at a small clearing, where grimy rocks formed a broken circle.

Teenagers drank in the clearing after dark. He kicked away their crushed beer cans, made as big a fire as he dared and squatted onto a scrap of cardboard. He put one hand over the fire, testing. He unzipped his parka, tossed it behind him, then stuck his flannel shirt sleeve into the flames. Fire whooshed a trail up his arm. He smacked wildly at the heat, then ripped off the shirt and stomped it into the blackened earth.

***

Suzie doesn't protest when I tell her to get her coat and boots because even though she complains a lot, she pretty much adores me. At least that's what my mother says.

We follow Robbie across the lane to his place. All the lights are on. I hear hooting and laughing. Robbie has a big family, so I'm not worried. Suzie and I scoot down the stairs to the basement. Robbie closes the door and follows us. All basements on the army base are pretty much the same — concrete walls and floor, empty except for a furnace and washing machine. Maybe an extra fridge under the stairs. Robbie has a ping-pong table, though. The hockey game is on the floor beside the table. He plops himself down cross-legged at the Montreal end, picks up the puck from centre ice and drops it. "Ready? Go!"

Robbie is good at this, and he wants to show off. It doesn't help that Suzie is distracting me by jumping over centre ice, barely clearing the game, her long red hair bouncing as she twirls and leaps back to the other side. "Can we go home, Bradley?" she asks every time she lands.

Two of Robbie's brothers lurch by us. "You found someone to play with, you little shit," one of them says, not unkindly, to Robbie. They grab the paddles on the ping-pong table and start smashing and spiking the ball. They're trying to hit the beer cans they've set up on either side of the net.

Suzie glares at them, then at me. It's time to leave. Robbie can tell I'm getting restless. "One more game, Brad. Ignore those rat finks."

An older boy I don't recognize, somebody from off the base, sways as he watches Robbie's brothers play, his chunky back to us. They're calling him Jimbo. I get to drop the puck this time and we start another game. Robbie sends the puck bumping past my goalie into the net.

"Jesus." Jimbo is holding Robbie's dad's rifle. "You guys got a gun?"

My stomach does a little flip. Most houses on the base have guns. My father keeps his in our basement too, and the bullets in his bureau drawer and the bolt someplace secret. We're never allowed to touch any of it.

"Watch, dudes." He crouches like Chuck Norris in *The Rifleman*.

"I want to go home, Bradley." Suzie speaks in a stage whisper. She's frowning at Jimbo, her lower lip stuck out.

"Shut up, Suzie." I concentrate on winning this game quickly so we can leave.

Someone lets off a firecracker, a loud one. At least that's what I think at first. I can't make the connection. Between the gun and the sound. Between the sound and Suzie twisting, turning to me in mid-air, a question in her eyes. The question might be: What was that noise? Or maybe: Why does my chest hurt so much? But she never gets to ask. She shoots backwards and falls against the edge of the ping-pong table. Then her head slams onto the cement floor. Jimbo's mouth is open. He's frozen, still aiming the rifle like Chuck Norris. Suzie's head is all crooked. Her hand flaps, then goes still.

***

His mother was in the kitchen with the radio blaring. The announcer sounded excited; the whole city was shutting down. Schools closing, cars abandoned in drifts, staff and customers having a sleepover at the Bay and Eaton's down town. Others shuttered in, hunkered down at home.

Another chance.

He lay on his bed, rummaging through the neighbourhood. Thought of the swings at the park just off the base behind the public school. His mother had made him take Suzie there on her birthday. He'd protested while Suzie flipped up the hood of her pink sweatshirt and tied her running shoes, excited. Leaves, browning on the trees and scuttling in the wind, chased them down the lane.

"Tell me a story, Bradley!" she shrieked as he pushed her higher and higher. The sun came out. Her shadow stretched in the dirt, then returned to him, solid and life-size. Away and back to him.

The swing set. Thick metal tripod legs at

either end, set into concrete. The top beam of the frame fifteen feet off the ground, at least. He was barely five feet tall. Two feet of snow from the blizzard. He reached under his bed, retrieved the thick rope coiled there, estimated distances and lengths, tied a slipknot at one end of the rope and left the other end loose.

Finally, ready. "Going for a walk, Mom," he said. "To see the snow." Almost surprised at how cheerful he sounded. How free he felt. At least part of him did. The other part was anxious about whether his plan would work.

His mother was pressing open a seam on his father's khaki uniform shirt. Steam hissed from the iron as she rested it upright on the ironing board. She smiled at him.

"You're ready to go back, aren't you? I'm glad."

It was the first Friday in March and the plan was for him to return to school Monday morning.

"Yup." Bradley averted his eyes.

"Big storm on its way. Don't stay out too long."

He scuffed through the shin-deep drifts, bowing to the wind. He fingered the thick rope he'd stuffed into the pocket of his parka. It felt soft but strong. At the park, he studied the towering green swing set and traced a route for his climb. They'd taken the swings and chains down for winter, which made his plan even easier to execute. He was excited now. A bit sick in his stomach, but happy. Ecstatic actually. He could hear his heart pumping in his ears. He shimmied up one of the thick metal legs, swung himself over the top beam and balanced there as though riding a horse. He hugged the cold metal with his arms and legs, pulling himself along on his stomach to the middle. It took all his strength and balance to stay on top instead of slinging underneath like the sloth at the zoo.

Now the hard part. He sat up straight on the crossbar, pulled off his mittens and threw them down.

Suzie had tried to speak to him. The words were too soft to understand. He leaned over and brought his ear to her mouth. He still couldn't make out what she was saying. A string of red hair stuck to her lips. Dots of blood dribbled out the side of her mouth, slid down her cheek. A bloodstain the shape of her heart grew and seeped across the front of her dressing gown. She lay still. Her eyes closed. One fuzzy slipper had fallen off. He wanted to press on her chest with his palms to stop the bleeding, but instead he stared, frozen, at the spreading red.

He took the rope out of his pocket, pulled down the hood of his parka with one hand, tested the slip knot again and put his head through the loop. He hooked the other end around the top beam, pulled it, then tied hitch knot after hitch knot to secure the right length of rope between the top beam and the knot around his neck.

He felt lighter and lighter.

A dog barked in the distance. Then stopped.

He leaned forward until his chest rested on cold metal. He relaxed his grip, ready to let go. The blizzard had erased the houses rimming the park, the school, the slide, the teeter-totter.

Nothing but whiteness all around.

Theresa Ann Wallace lives in Old Ottawa East. She worked as a freelance researcher, writer, editor and communications consultant for close to four decades. Her writing has been published in newspapers and national magazines. In 2014, she began to devote her time to the writing of short fiction and creative non-fiction. She placed second in the inaugural *Ottawa Magazine* short story contest and won the 2017 Capital Crime Writers short story contest.

Judge's Comment

This story has a masterful use of descriptive detail and the writer has calm control of the overall story arc. The lines are cool but not cold. They observe and relate. The four elements abide throughout the story and are picked up again and again. The story is filled with sensory detail and the human relationships within are nuanced. It is a deeply sad and affecting story that wouldn't leave me. Heartbreaking.

SECOND PLACE SHORT STORY

P. R. ISFELD

CHATTER

My best friend Lila Wilson lived in a big ranch style house on the outside of town. In 1980 we bonded over *Tiger Beat* magazines and infatuation with Leif Garrett and Shaun Cassidy. We imagined ourselves sisters, somehow separated at birth. But her father was a banker and mine was a traveling drug salesman, so there were important differences between us.

Her dad sat down to dinner with his family every night, leaving his job behind downtown. My dad worked from home sometimes, but then blasted off in his car, headed for the airport or the open highway. Once a year, Mr. Wilson escorted Lila to the bank for "Take Your Daughters to Work Day." Every summer, my dad took me on a weeklong road trip in his black GTO.

"One law, Miss Patricia," he said that July as we packed our bags into the capacious trunk and settled into the leather seats. .

"What?" I said. Asking was part of the game, since the rule never changed. Dad liked to repeat himself like a Catskills comedian. I was happy to play along since I knew the trip almost hadn't happened that summer. Dad drove less and less those days, preferring to spend his travel allowance to fly and rent cars on arrival.

He smiled, pleased I knew my part. "No touching anything."

"Aye -aye."

"Especially the CB," he continued, pointing to the two-way radio on the dashboard. "We might need it in an emergency." Then he deepened his voice and intoned: "Fasten your seatbelts and prepare for liftoff." The V-8 engine sprang to life, and we were off.

This particular day took us west along the Trans-Canada, headed for Thunder Bay, where Dad had set up a few days' worth of calls. I watched the traffic and the road signs and the exit ramps cycle by. My father smoked Players, holding the cigarette below the open window, but every now and then the wind sent ashes whirling inside the car. He grinned as he approached one of the big long-distance trucks from behind, then pulled around it and gunned the muscle car's engine, earning a filthy look — and a raised middle finger — from the trucker. His rig had a red, grinning skull painted on the side. By afternoon I had stretched out on the back seat, letting the warm air swirl above me, listening to the static on the CB. Sometimes the hisses and pops sounded like a message.

The clouds on the darkening horizon were just beginning to look bruised when I woke up. Dad told me I'd been sleeping so well he'd decided to push on to Sault Ste Marie rather than stopping in Sudbury for the night. We'd had a late start because of my mom's insistence on feeding us "a proper lunch" before we left. I enjoyed the red glow of the dashboard, the few lonely headlights passing in the other direction, the skeletal outlines of trees against the horizon, and every so often, the flash of wild eyes in the ditch.

The CB crackled like a fire pit. Mounted under the dashboard, the silver machine had a small knob that powered it on and controlled the volume, a UHF display with a red needle that jumped as it got a signal, a big dial for changing the channel, and a bright green display that showed its frequency. We kept ours on nineteen, the trucker channel, since Dad said that was where more people would be listening most of the time. The red needle bounced with every burst of chatter.

"Can I try another channel?" I asked, reaching for the dial.

"Don't, leave it, there" said Dad, exhaling smoke. "Nineteen is the one we can rely on to tell us what's ahead. You never know what's on those other ones."

I knew better than to argue. On previous trips, Dad had let me use the CB to ask for directions or get news on the traffic situation farther up the road, but he seemed to have forgotten about that. Wind blew through the open window and lifted a flurry of grey flakes from the overstuffed ashtray. Dad chain-smoked with grim determination on the road. At home, Mom wouldn't let him light up inside the house, so he sat with our border collie on the back porch, the two of them watching the headlights on the distant highway.

I flapped my hands at him. "Dad, you're getting cigarette crap all over me."

He grinned and ground the butt into the ashtray. "Sorry," he said, ruffling my hair. "Okay?" His hand bumped my head, his big gold signet ring rough against my forehead.

"Smoking is bad for you," I said.

"You're right."

"Lila's father doesn't."

I felt his sideways glance. "Doesn't what?"

"Smoke."

"Yeah? Well, you probably have no idea what he does when Lila's mom isn't looking. Besides, Lila's faaaatha"—he drew out the last word—"isn't out here on the road. I work for a living."

"He works." I thought of Mr. Wilson's neat little suits and ring-less hands.

"Sitting in an air-conditioned office saying no to people you've known your whole life isn't working." He jerked his thumb at the red binder on the back seat. "Open that up. You'll see my logs of every call I make, and every sale I get. I know where every cent that feeds you and your mom came from. Can Wilson show Lila anything like that?"

"I don't know, Daddy," I said, chastened. "All I'm saying is he doesn't smoke."

"No, Patricia, you said a lot more than that." He grabbed the half-empty pack of Player's off the dashboard and whipped it into the back seat. By the time we slowed for the next exit ramp, twenty minutes of silence had stretched between us. Dad looked over at me.

"We need gas. There's still a whole lotta nothing between us and the Soo."

I nodded. Better not to talk when he was mad.

He pulled past the truck stop and up to the well-lit gas pumps, skillfully maneuvering the GTO in a circle so the tank was on the right side. Silence closed in as soon as the engine stopped. I jumped out, grabbing the squeegee from the bucket beside the hoses, and dragged it across the windshield with both hands. A line of grungy truck-stop water ran down my forearms.

Dad finished gassing up. "You want anything from inside?" he asked.

"Nah, I'll go to the washroom and meet you back here," I said. Truck stop restaurants grossed me out and besides, I wasn't ready to make it easy for him. I made a show of reaching into the car, pulling out the ashtray, and dumping the butts into the garbage.

"Suit yourself," he said, walking slowly toward the building. "Don't forget to check the back seat and lock the doors when you come back."

I got back from the washroom quickly. There were a few benefits to being a girl at a truck stop. Once inside the car, I ducked down and, with a defiant glance at Dad as he stood in line at the cashier, broke his only rule.

The CB microphone felt like a rock in my hand. Feedback squawked from the transmitter, and I turned the volume down. It still burped static, softly.

Through the windshield I could see my father about to pay. The interior of the truck stop gleamed like an operating theatre and the wall clock read just after midnight. Dad left the counter with a newspaper tucked under his arm and I knew he was heading for the washroom.

I lifted the mike, switched the channel, and pressed the talk key. "Breaker one-five," I said, my voice sounding high and thin over the sandpapery static.

Immediate response: "Go ahead break one-five."

On the CB, everyone identified themselves by handles, invented names often intended to be humorous, or boastful, or both. I'd listened to Lead Foot, Screaming Eagle, and Harry Ball earlier that night. I went by Scout, from the heroine of my favourite novel, *To Kill a Mockingbird.* My dad liked the name since it didn't identify me as a girl. This guy called himself Black Dog. He had a Quebecois accent, common among truckers, but his sounded weird.

"Are you good tonight Scout?"

I held the mike close to my lips, and deepened my voice, hoping to disguise my age. "Ten-four."

There were two or three other conversations on the channel. Their transmissions faded in and out as vehicles passed through the CB's four-mile range.

"Haven't seen any smokies tonight," said Black Dog. "A good night for road-running."

"Copy that," I said.

The speakers warbled and suddenly a deep, clear voice broke in. "Get off the channel, kid."

The crunch of footsteps on the gravel outside made me straighten up in my seat, I relaxed when I saw not my dad but a fat trucker in Doc Martins, faded blue jeans and an AC/DC t-shirt. He crossed in front of the GTO, heading for the truck stop from the diesel pumps. His long dark hair trailed behind him in a ponytail.

"What's your ten-twenty?" asked Black Dog.

"We're headed for Sault—"

"Get off the channel, kid. Stop talking to yourself."

"But I'm not—" I started.

Black Dog interrupted, sounding pissed off. "Don't let them bug you. Switch over to twenty-seven and call out." Then he was gone.

The parking lot was silent. Outside the glare of the floodlights over the pumps, the darkness stretched back forever. I could make out the shapes of a few parked vehicles, but the truck stop looked deserted. I turned the dial to twenty-seven. Silence. I turned up the volume.

Suddenly, I felt guilty. Maybe I shouldn't be doing this after all. I released the key, and the small metallic click sounded on the channel.

The transmission arrived like a clap of thunder. "Break twenty-seven for Scout."

Maybe if I stayed quiet, he'd think I'd moved out of range.

"Scouuuuut," he said, his voice wheedling and insistent. Only later would I realize that his French accent had vanished. "I can hear your breath, Scout. Come out, come out, wherever you are."

I looked at the clock above the cashier. Twelve fifteen. More than ten minutes had passed, and Black Dog's voice remained clear, showing that he was still inside the CB's small range. I wasn't moving and neither was he.

Turn it off, I told myself, staring at the black, perforated surface of the microphone. The speakers buzzed like insects.

The voice came through again. Still crisp and clear. "Is that you in the passenger seat, Scout?"

I sat up and looked wildly around. Three bays down, just beyond the floodlights, I could make out an old semi-trailer behind the diesel pumps. Inside its dark cab the scarlet point of a cigarette glowed, then disappeared.

"This your daddy's nice car? That his book with the address on the front? You don't want to talk on the radio, maybe I can pay you a visit."

He must have looked in the back seat while I was in the washroom. If he knew where my dad worked, he could find me. What if I annoyed him and he got out of the cab right now? Could I run to the truck stop fast enough?

"Want to know something, Scout?"

I stared at the mike, helpless.

"What do you see when you close your eyes? When you look out past the lights, what do you think is there? Nothing. Yet. But I see you. Every time you look into the night, it stares back at you. "

Black Dog's voice was a poisonous gas inside the car. I wanted to run away but wasn't sure which direction to go. Better to stay put. At least there was a locked door between us.

"I'm watching your daddy, Scout. I'm patient. We're out on the same highway, clocking the same miles. He thinks he can outrun me in his fancy car. One of these days he'll open his eyes and look into the night and see me. He's only got so many miles and—"

Enough. I slammed the mike into its cradle and turned off the radio. My breath sounded ragged. I closed my eyes, then heard gravel crunch beside the car.

"No!" I shouted, sitting bolt upright.

"Whoa, a little nightmare there?" Dad stood outside the driver's door, smiling, our earlier tension forgotten. A few minutes apart did wonders for the attitude. Grinning back, I reached over to pop the lock. He got in, dropping a copy of the latest *Tiger Beat* between the seats.

"Touch anything?" he asked. A routine question, requiring the same routine answer.

"Nope."

He turned the key and the powerful engine throbbed. He pulled away from the pump and guided the GTO toward the highway, gliding between the diesel pumps on our way out. I looked over toward the black outline of the old semi-trailer, and caught the red-orange glow of another cigarette and — maybe I imagined it — the outline of a skull on the side panel.

And then Black Dog was out of range.

We reached cruising speed in the middle lane and Dad reached for the dashboard. He turned on the CB and changed the channel back to nineteen, saying nothing. Soon I heard the click of a lighter and smelled the scent of burning tobacco, but I said nothing either. Occasionally he coughed or one of us reached into the bag of jellybeans he had propped on the dashboard. He didn't comment on the way I stared at the rearview mirror, searching for the lights of a semi-trailer behind us, intent on running us off the road. We made it to the Soo and our hotel room. I felt as if I had been awake for days.

Despite my exhaustion, I slept fitfully in my twin bed, listening to my father snore. When I got up to go to the bathroom in the blue early morning light, I looked down at him. He was asleep with his mouth open, snoring, the thin white motel sheet draped over his distended belly. Little black hairs like ants dotted his chin.

I tore my eyes away immediately, feeling like I shouldn't be spying on him. Seeing him asleep was not new, but I have never been able to erase that particular pre-dawn image from my mind. Even though it was more five years — and a half-dozen father-daughter road trips — before he died clutching his chest at a Belleville truck stop, he looked like a corpse already.

Judge's Comment

The story begins quietly enough as a study of a father–daughter relationship and quickly becomes menacing as the narrator interacts with an untethered voice on the CB. Floating in space, the threatening voice pulls the narrator back to the here/now and unsettles her. It ends with the quiet disturbing image of the sleeping father, an image which is both tender and wary, that captures the reader.

P. R. Isfeld has spent more than twenty years in the federal government, seeking refuge from bureaucracy by writing fiction. Although she moved to the National Capital Region toward the end of the last century, she has never lost her love of the CB radios and long road-trips that were part of her prairie childhood.

THIRD PLACE, SHORT STORY

SUZY ROYLE

FRUIT

Annabel watches her mother-in-law remove the wrapping paper without tearing it and open the large cardboard box. Out floats a pale blue balloon, curled ribbons trailing like tentacles. Ginny's head tilts back as the balloon saunters up to the living room ceiling, its gleaming belly proclaiming *IT'S A BO !* in sans-serif glitter.

Annabel surveys the upturned faces of her husband's family.

"Boy. It's supposed to be *BOY.* The Y rubbed off," she says.

Everyone starts talking, but the only voice Annabel hears is Ginny's:

"Well. Isn't that ... something."

It is. It's something Annabel and Brent thought would delight his mother to no end, she a grandmother to nine-year-old twin girls.

Ginny's eyes burn into Annabel's twenty-one-week bump, as though trying to see for herself. Annabel's stomach contracts in a futile attempt to suck in. Her cheeks grow hot and she suddenly doesn't know where to put her hands.

Ginny's focus leaps to Annabel's face. Her mouth smiles without her eyes' consent.

"Congratulations. Once again. You must be just ecstatic."

She is. Brent too. It isn't every day that a couple gets pregnant — *naturally* — after countless years of trying. After being branded broken — on both sides. After giving up.

Actually, Annabel isn't ecstatic. She would have been five, seven years ago. But to be five months pregnant with a healthy baby boy at forty-one? She is well beyond the bounds of ecstasy.

Annabel plays nice. "We are." She smiles at her mother-in-law and slides a hand onto her belly. Like armour.

Having suffered numerous miscarriages, Annabel and Brent initially told no one, their expectations low, bruised from years of disappointment. With each week, the dread grew more and more faint, until it was replaced by burgeoning hope. They waited twelve weeks, plus two more to be safe, before they shared their good fortune.

Annabel longed to tell her parents in person and feel their joyful embrace, but with them in Saskatoon, she had to settle for Skype. Her mother screamed and her father wept. She expected something similar from Brent's parents. Minus the tears. Brent's dad never cries. "My mom will," Brent promised.

They arrived unannounced at Brent's parents' house one Saturday afternoon in March. Ginny made tea and they settled onto stools around the kitchen island. Annabel plucked a lemon from the fruit bowl and placed it in the centre of the butcher block top.

"We thought you'd like to see how big your grandchild is."

"Our what?" Brent's father, Harry, squinted and pitched his good ear forward.

"*Grandchild,*" Brent said. "Anna's pregnant."

"Really? That's ... *wow.*" He went and stood between Annabel and Brent, pulling them into him.

"Well, you certainly don't look it. Still early days, I take it."

"Fourteen weeks. The risk is much lower now — that's why we waited to tell you."

"We've come a long way," Brent said. "I mean, to think it started out as a microscopic speck, and now it's this big?" He palmed the lemon and cradled it in his hand. "That's pretty astounding."

They all considered the lemon.

"Aren't you leaving it a bit late?" Ginny finally spoke.

Brent's face went slack.

"The risks, I mean." Ginny levelled her eyes onto Annabel. "Is having a baby at your age a responsible thing to do?"

Suzy Royle started writing at age eight, when her teacher assigned story writing and published the results into handmade books. She has an Honours English degree and a diploma in print journalism. She has previously won and placed in the National Capital Writing Contest. Her work has been published in the *Ottawa Citizen*, *The Globe and Mail*, and in several anthologies. She was born in Toronto and grew up in eastern Canada. She now lives in Perth, Ontario.

Judge's Comment

My favourite image from this story is that of the announcement balloon, curving its way out of its box like some sort of sea creature, with its missing glitter letter. The fruit at the title is a common image with pregnant women, one that allows them to envision their baby in various forms of produce as the pregnancy progresses. The story unwinds around family tensions and circles back, ending after a stillbirth with the loneliest image of the mother anticipating something that never does come. It is a story of absence and loss.

"Mom!" Brent barked. "After all we've been through. If you can't be happy for us then you can just—"

"Fuck off." Annabel said it so he didn't have to.

They left without another word. Harry tried to block the door. "C'mon now, let' s talk this through. We all say things we don't mean."

Only, they did.

They spent the next seven weeks attempting to claw their way back to the easy relationship they'd enjoyed before. It was a slow slog. And they weren't even close. Annabel saw the damage — on both sides — as irreparable, but was willing to try for Brent's sake.

Flowers were sent, both to and from, testing waters.

Dawn, Brent's sister, came bearing fruit. Literally. And well-thumbed pregnancy and child-rearing books, plus a jumbo container of pre-natal vitamins that had Ginny written all over it. Down to the yellow self-adhesive bow.

There were tentative phone calls, trial meetings on neutral territory with Dawn' s girls providing a buffer. A convenient reminder to get along for the sake of the baby.

Things grew easier around the time Annabel's amniocentesis results came back clear. Proof Ginny's efforts were indeed warranted, Annabel figured. As if a grandmother needed prompting.

So Annabel unclenched her jaw and adopted a new mantra: *happy. family. happy. family.*

Inhale *happy.* Exhale *family.*

Annabel leans back into the couch, hand still on her paunch as though she has eaten too much pie. One of the twins shoves the balloon under her shirt and rubs her impressive girth. It looks alarmingly realistic.

Dawn shimmies it free. "Careful, honey. We don't want to pop it." Harry sinks down next to Annabel.

"No fruit this time?"

"Couldn't find anything blue enough." She smiles.

"A boy." Harry grins, lines fanning from cheek to temple. He pats her hand. "It's been a long time."

"Can I get you something to eat?" Ginny asks, the tips of her ivory loafers kissing Annabel's bare toes.

"I'm fine, thanks." Annabel remembers to smile.

Ginny cocks her head and says in a sing-song, "Don't forget, you're eating for two now."

"True, but one of us is the size of—"

"Let me guess ... a grapefruit?" Harry says.

"Papaya. According to my pregnancy app."

"You don't say." He shakes his head.

"Well, whatever the size, the only way it's going to eat is if you do. I'm getting you a snack."

Ginny is gone before Annabel can correct her.

He.

***

Ginny and Dawn are standing back-on at the kitchen sink as Annabel approaches with her empty plate. She has dutifully polished off the small mound of veggies and hummus Ginny produced.

"She must know the risks," Ginny says, her voice barely audible above the swishing dishwater. "I mean her age is just the beginning."

Annabel hides behind the wall.

"You'd think ..." Dawn said.

"With all they've been through ... And autism rates are higher in boys. Even higher in boys with older fathers. I read that online. If I were them, I wouldn't exactly be celebrating."

"Try to be happy for them, Mom. It's been a long road."

"Exactly. They've got a long road ahead of them still. I won't be able to relax and enjoy this baby until it's at least one or two, once it's walking, talking, and we can be sure there's nothing wrong with it."

Annabel doesn't hurl her plate against the wall. Or at Ginny's head. She places it on the hall table and develops a sudden case of overwhelming fatigue. She manages to extricate her husband without having to speak to his mother.

In the car, Brent asks what's wrong.

"Just tired." Annabel averts her head, darting her eyes back and forth to stave off oncoming tears. "I expected your mom to be more excited."

"Oh, she will be. Give her time."

One to two years, perhaps.

The technician squirts gel onto Annabel's exposed belly and spreads it with the probe as though icing a cake. Annabel catches Brent's eye and smiles. He squeezes her hand.

This is their mid-pregnancy "anomaly" ultrasound. In which they ... scan for anomalies, Annabel supposes. She doesn't really know. Her amnio was clear, she's surpassed the halfway mark ... This scan is gravy. Numbers to plug into her chart, another box to check off.

Through murk and cloud-like haze, he appears on screen. Their son. Head hulking over tiny limbs curled towards his heart.

"There he is," the technician sings. She turns a dial and the room is awash in a rushing sound.

"Is that his heartbeat?" Brent asks.

"No, the placenta."

She slides the probe north, then south. More clouds and fuzz.

"Hey, where'd he go?" Annabel says.

"Sorry." The tech lifts the probe and replaces it, glides right, then left. "I'm just looking for ..." She presses downward, as though making an impression, then grinds it like a heel into Annabel's softest part.

"Just a sec, okay?" the technician says. "Technical issues."

She turns the sound off and leaves the room, returning with a man in a white coat. He watches the screen as the tech darts the probe around Annabel's stomach.

Finally, their baby reappears, in the same sweet position as before. His spine is an upside-down question mark, arrayed in white pebbles. Is that his thumb in his mouth?

The tech wipes the head of the probe and replaces it in its holster. The man introduces himself as a radiologist.

"I'm sorry to have to tell you this, but we can't find a heartbeat."

"What do you mean, you can't find it? Keep looking." Annabel whips around for confirmation, but finds the screen blank.

"There is no heartbeat. Your baby died. I'm so sorry."

No. Annabel's eyes run to Brent. He isn't buying this either.

"But she said there were technical problems," Brent says. "Can— Can' t we try another machine?"

"It would have the same result, I'm afraid. I am terribly sorry."

Annabel's vision bulges and blurs as though her eyes have also been smeared with that gel. Tears squeeze their way onto her cheeks and she can see again.

Annabel closes her eyes.

Sight, hearing — any of the senses, speech, organs, fun ... Joy, because that's forever lost to her now too ... Annabel keeps a mental tally of all the things she would trade for her baby's life. She would gladly trade her own. Why couldn't she have simply died giving birth? That would have been so much cleaner and just. A life for a life. No bystanders left to mourn away the rest of their pathetic existences.

They were given the choice of inducing the birth or having the baby surgically removed — like a tumour, or something. Annabel refuses to abort their baby, dead or alive.

Brent and Annabel return to the hospital the next day, equally distraught and disbelieving. They are given a private room where Annabel lies, allowing induction drugs to flood her veins, instigating the expulsion of her baby, whom she felt kicking only days earlier. She fantasizes about tearing the needle from her arm and fleeing to the woods. Her son could stay within her, and if she died, well, at least they would never be separated.

Annabel sighs. Brent fields texts from family and weeps without sound. It's like someone has muted him. Annabel cries until she can't.

When the contractions begin, Annabel is offered narcotics. She accepts.

Soon after she is handed the dose controller ("whenever you feel pain, just press that button"), distant thunder growls, as though Annabel produced it with a press of the little blue button. She isn't yet ready to explore the myriad ways she may have caused her baby to die. That will come.

The nurse arrives to check on them. A freckled woman with a tender voice.

"Painkillers cross the placenta, don't they? I don't want to harm my baby." A peal of thunder sounds overhead.

The corners of the nurse's mouth dig into her cheeks. "Our priority right now is you."

Of course. Her baby can't get any more dead.

Another thunderclap. The lights flicker. It's like a bad movie. "Don't worry, we're on a generator," the nurse says.

The contractions intensify and grow closer together. Annabel thumbs the blue button. She feels pressure, but no pain. Excitement surges — she will meet her baby soon. Then she remembers.

Objects in the room lurch and leer. Again, it's as though she has gel or Vaseline smeared on her eyeballs. Only this time she isn't crying.

Everything seems poorly lit and cast in shadow, despite fluorescent bulbs and daylight pushing its way through the window. Like she's living inside her cell phone with the brightness turned down.

The pregnancy books didn't mention this part.

Annabel shuts her eyes against it. Against Brent's face that she can't bear to see.

The thunder continues. So do the contractions. At times, they synchronize, the sonorous double bass *BOOM!* reverberating at the crest of the wave, giving Annabel the impression she is performing a fated, choreographed version of her life.

She opens her eyes long enough to glimpse a flash of mauve tinting the sky. A wash of violet watercolour. Purple as a blossoming bruise.

The baby is born in three pushes. Brent's hand shakes as he cuts the umbilical cord. The only sound is that of his sobs, bunching and overlapping as he gasps for air.

Annabel has watched dozens of birth videos, witnessing the screeching entrances of countless babies.

This isn't right. It's too quiet.

Finally, Annabel sees her son, swaddled into a tiny flannel bundle.

The nurse places him in Annabel's arms. This is where the new parents are congratulated.

After a moment, the nurse murmurs, "He's beautiful."

Annabel nods. Brent's sobs escalate.

He *is* beautiful. Perfect. All the things a new baby can be. But motionless. And so, so silent.

He weighs almost nothing. Annabel has held heavier mangoes.

She wonders about the colour of his eyes but can't bring herself to lift his eyelid. She envisions the skin tearing like wet tissue paper. And his unseeing eyes would proclaim Death. With his eyes closed, he could just be sleeping.

"Take as much time as you need," the nurse says.

They are left alone. Brent climbs onto the narrow bed and lies with his arm cradling Annabel's arm that cradles their son. They name him Samuel Harry. Brent's breathing regulates. The thunder subdues as the storm retreats.

Annabel will not be relinquishing her baby. Not until he is pulled from her arms. She will hold him every second she can, knowing a time will come when she would trade a limb for one minute more.

Brent's phone dings.

"Mom's downstairs. She has flowers."

Annabel doesn't respond.

"Anna?"

"I don't care if she has the Hope Diamond."

Her eyes don't leave her baby. She doesn't have much time to cram in decades of loving.

Annabel hears Brent type. "What are you saying?"

"That you're not ready. You need more time."

Eternity, maybe.

Annabel's eyes roam Samuel's face. Her hand burrows into the swaddle to memorize his body. She uncovers a minuscule hand and stifles the urge to mould his translucent fringe of fingers around her pinkie. Instead, she gingerly encloses it in her own.

Annabel's ears are pricked for the approach of the person who will take him. She needs something else to listen for, but there is nothing. Not the arrival of her mother-in-law. Not her husband's sobs. Not the breath of her sleeping baby.

So she listens for the rain.

But it never does come.

HONOURABLE MENTION

JOAN McKAY

Joan McKay says poetry is her first love. She believes that every creative act, no matter the medium, has the potential to change our world. She has been a frequent winner in the Canadian Authors' Association annual NCWC contest, a finalist in Malahat's Long Poem contest, and won the Irish Comórtais Liteartha for poetry in Irish in the Diaspora. Joan lives in Kingston, Ontario, where she enjoys taking yoga classes and studying Irish Gaelic and Italian.

MEERKAT

*Meerkat: a small southern African mongoose. They are very aware of their surroundings and always on the lookout for potential threats and predators.

Miriam surveyed the array of small cereal boxes on the table in front of her, settled on frosted flakes with their dusting of icing sugar. "Sorry," she whispered to rice crispies who rocked forward ominously and to the others who tilted ever so slightly to one side, "maybe tomorrow."

She heard her father's sigh. "Meerkat, stop your nonsense."

Even though he used his pet name for her, she knew enough to stop.

"He doesn't understand." She whispered the words inside her head and felt the faint vibration as the boxes nodded in agreement. He hadn't understood either when the big tree in the back yard cried for a week when he screwed a big bolt for a clothesline into its body. She'd sat beside it, her face pressed against its rough bark, trying to soothe its pain for the entire week. She'd taken her cereal bowl outside and perched under its leafy canopy. "There, there," she'd said, moving her hands along its rough body. The crying grew less loud and she'd known she was helping.

Gradually the weeping became a whimper and one day it disappeared altogether. She began having her breakfast inside again. Her father started giving her a funny look she didn't understand. The look made her uncomfortable. At first she thought he, too, had been concerned about maple tree. But something inside her rejected the thought almost the moment it occurred to her. No, if he'd known the pain he would cause, surely he wouldn't have done it. But he had done it, to the helpless tree, to the tiny ants he swept unceremoniously off the counter.

***

Miriam loved visiting the Museum of Natural History. While her brothers imagined being in armed combat with the dinosaurs, she imagined curling up in the vast basket of a dinosaur's ribcage and being rocked by its lumbering movement across the savanna of its homeland. She imagined summer heat, the stillness of night, being rocked back to a different beginning, to being born as something large enough to be seen, large enough to shatter silence, loud enough to be heard.

Her father's hand on her shoulder, urging her to move on to the next exhibit, branded her skin. She could feel the blistering through her shirt. She imagined she was a gazelle, leaping through long grass, the weightlessness of air, becoming invisible in the dazzling light.

***

In her dream, her hands were held by long spikes — like Jesus on the cross, the way she'd seen him pinned to the wall in the big church she had ventured into one day when her sadness needed a place to rest. The church smelled of wood polish and of the melting wax from dozens of candles in small red glasses. She sat for a long time on one of the hard benches, listening to the music coming from each of the hymn books stored on the back of the pews. It started very softly, then grew louder, wound itself around her legs, up her body and along the back of the seat. In a sudden rush it jumped to the nearest pillar and shot to the top, then slid down the other side in a descending scale. She felt her sadness lifting as the melody ran back up the next pillar and slid smoothly along the ceiling. It was only when the music climbed back into the books and became quiet that she got up to leave. She looked again at the candles in the corner. Like a giant birthday cake, the light flickered on currents of air. But in the glow, the wax appeared to be the same colour as the drops of blood on Jesus' hands.

At breakfast the next morning, Miriam kept looking at her own hands, hoping no one would notice. She couldn't tell them about the dream. She couldn't tell anyone about the dream.

***

Outside, after breakfast, she became a yellow kite, yellow as the sun. She flew higher and higher, closer and closer to the light, until she was swallowed by its heat, burned to ash, and floated in a million pieces to the sea below. The pieces rested on the cool surface, a sparkle of promises about to sink into the depths where no one would ever find them.

Judge's Comment

I appreciated this story's unusual perspective and imagery which expressed the narrator's voice so clearly. It has a uniquely imagistic voice which suited the narrator's personification of the inanimate, her blossoming uncertainty and her disjuncture in the more narrative world. Like her namesake the meerkat, she keeps her eyes open and has a wide range of vision. I appreciate the poetic quality of the lines throughout this story.

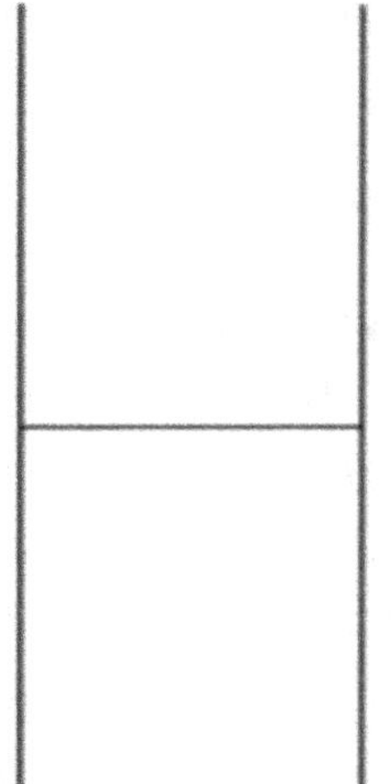

HONOURABLE MENTION

MAR PRESTON

THE 600-MILE ENDING

That kind of Northern Ontario rain is almost sleet, a mournful drizzle that chills the bones. The weather report predicted a steep drop in temperature. Running low on gas, the red truck we'd spent our last money on sent out choking drifts of black smoke.

My father had said, "Why in hell do youse want to go way up north there? There's nothing up there but trees. And that damn truck you're driving isn't safe. You blow a tire and there's nobody for fifty miles. I'm tellin' you." He got up off the chesterfield and humphed out of the room, muttering, and slammed the back door.

"Oh, Dad, we'll be fine," I called after him, intent on showing my new American boyfriend the wilds of northern Ontario. Invincible, bullet-proof and arrogant with the power of being young, both of us excited for adventure. A city boy from Los Angeles, everything was new to Brett. Canada was a foreign country, a little backward there in the '70s. I heard him on the phone laughing with one of his friends back in LA that now we had paved roads and flush toilets. Both Dad and I noticed Brett was spooked by the dark and the silence of Dad's place on the edge of town.

Last night after a long day of seeing a lot of trees and not much else, we checked into a cardboard shack motel room that cost $30. For hours, the couple next door banged the headboard against the wall, playing porn loud. I had discovered by then that Brett liked skin mags and women with ballooning breasts. Neither of us wanted to brave the bathroom with its threadbare towels in the morning, so we set off grubby and sleepless. The gas station sold coffee. Nothing else was open. The thermometer registered 10 below. The gas was so expensive, we decided to chance it till we got to Hearst, one of the bigger towns on the TransCanada Highway, a couple of hours away. The sun hadn't lifted behind the trees yet. The headlights peered ahead into the darkness of near dawn. No radio reception this far north.

Our plan was to make a wide 600-mile round trip on Highway 11 heading north from the nickel mining city of Sudbury, looping east through an endless corridor of snow and black trees on a ribbon of pavement. The road crews had blasted rock cuts through the Laurentian Shield, miles of granite, capping much of eastern Ontario and Quebec. Some of the rock cuts were a hundred feet high, narrowing the blowing snow through steep canyons of roadway now covered with snow. We passed through scattered towns miles apart, most of the businesses shut up for the winter, one café, one gas station, and the Ontario Provincial Police station. A couple of streets of houses, looking cold and hunched, led off the main road. I took the next shift, driving slow, watching for black ice. The last thing I wanted to do was hit a moose.

Trees. More trees.

Peering through the mist rising off the pavement I saw what I thought was a human form draped over a rock by the side of the road. Slowly it assembled itself into an Indian kid dressed in a jeans jacket, jeans, and rubber boots. He lifted an arm, thumb out, as we neared.

Brett pulled himself upright from dozing, his head against the window "What are you doing?"

"He must be freezing. Look at him."

"He's Indian. He probably has a knife."

"I can't believe you," I said, wheeling around to look at him. "Did you just say that? Look, this is Canada. We're not in LA anymore."

"Don't do this. Don't stop. I'm telling you, don't do this."

"Look, we haven't seen another car in the last hour. He'll freeze to death."

Brett crossed his arms over his chest and looked out the window, not at me.

I halted the car next to the kid who was on the other side of the road. He pulled himself upright as if he were eighty years old and lumbered across the road to loom into my window. He brought with him a gust of stale beer breath, and bad teeth. I thought of what I knew of life on the rez. Fifty miles to the nearest grocery store, short growing season for gardens, lot of bannock bread and tea. Maybe some fish, game, some wild rice if his family was ambitious. Lot of Cree hired out as guides or did whatever seasonal work they could. There weren't a lot of businesses back there in the trees.

"Where you going?" I asked him.

He mumbled something. English? French? What? I hadn't been home from Los Angeles long enough to remember whether the kid was going to be Anishinabe or Cree. That was as far as my knowledge went, like most white people.

He swung a hand in a leather work glove

forward in the direction we were going.

"Hey, what's your name? What are you doin' out here? You must be pretty cold."

"Lloyd."

That I understood.

"He's not getting in front," Brett hissed, snapping the locks and leaning against the passenger door. I thought about it. I could let this one go.

"He can ride in back then," I said.

"What about our stuff?" he said.

"Just because he's Indian doesn't make him a thief."

I glared at Brett and told the kid to climb in the back. I watched him try to heave himself up, getting ready to get out and swing down the tailgate for him. He finally got a leg over the edge of the bed of the truck and fell into the back amongst our camping gear, food, and books. The truck, which had been idling, stalled. The clutch was about gone and the accelerator had a nervous touch. Tap it and the engine would stall.

"Sonofabtiching piece of shit," Brett said, slamming a fist down on the dashboard.

"You picked it. At least the heater works."

I spotted my purse in the back and thought about getting out to bring it in the truck. Brett flung himself out the door and yanked out his camera bag, his Bowie knife, and brought them back inside. He could have brought my purse but he didn't think of it.

Brett, fuming beside me, I cranked the truck into life again and we spluttered along. The snow was piling up on the roadway and the four-cylinder engine was struggling. I had one eye on the road ahead, and Lloyd in the back. He huddled up close to the window. I drove, one eye on the kid in the back, one eye watching the edge of the road so we wouldn't hit the snowbanks. We hadn't seen oncoming traffic since we'd left the motel.

Lloyd was rummaging in our belongings and pulled a tarp over himself.

"Look what he's doing," Brett said.

"Jesus, Brett, it's freezing out there. Your stuff's okay."

"You know how much that backpack cost me?"

Shut my mouth. We'd both been naïve when I asked Brett to come back to Ontario with me. Immigration wasn't quite as easy as we thought. We had a choice. Get married, or take a job working under the table. Brett refused to work for minimum wage. He was working on a novel.

"Whose bright idea was this trip anyway?" Brett complained, spinning the radio dial in the hopeless attempt to get radio reception.

"Yours as much as mine as I remember."

"Did you eat the last of the chips?" he said.

"No, you did. Don't start, please. I'm hungry too. We'll eat when we get to Hearst. There's food in the back ..."

"Don't even think about stopping ..." he interrupted. "And we're not paying for this guy's breakfast."

I glanced in back. I couldn't drive more than thirty miles an hour which meant it would take us another two hours to Hearst.

The tarp was covered with snow. I was now driving in a whiteout. Everything I knew about northern Ontario winter said pull over and wait for it to stop snowing. I looked for a turnout.

"What're you doing?"

I pulled the truck off the road into a flat staging area for the road crews where the snowplows left twelve-foot berms when they turned around to do the other side of the road. A snow hump made a perfect muffin top on top of the equipment shed.

No movement from the back of the truck. The green tarp with three inches of snow on it was still.

Brett and I looked at each other. Now I'd get the silent treatment for stopping, but he surprised me. I grabbed my gloves, pulling on my parka to look in the back. We opened both doors and got out, stumbling with the force of the wind and blowing snow.

I pulled the tarp off the kid lying under it. This kind of cold and his wet clothes could have frozen on him.

No movement. He was huddled into a fetal position hands between his thighs, shoulders hunched, eyes closed.

"Hey, Lloyd! Wake up now. Tell us where you're going?"

No answer. The snow swirled around us, deadening sound. A single light shone into the darkness from the equipment shed.

"What's the matter with him? He's not moving." Brett poked him hard.

A crust of snow had frozen on the boy's scanty beard and eyebrows. I shook him by the shoulder. He didn't move.

"Is he dead? Is he dead? He's dead. I know he's dead. What're we gonna do?" Brett said. He was dancing around next to me, his voice jagged and hysterical.

I thought he was dead too. I climbed up into the bed of the truck and pushed the kid up to a sitting position. He fell over sideways. Brett was right beside me inside the truck, jittering.

"They'll blame us."

"Who?"

"The police. That's what police do."

"This isn't LA, Brett."

"Look, let's just roll him out into the snowbank and leave him. We gotta get out of here."

"Are you actually serious? Just dump him?"

"He's dead. What does he care?"

"I thought I knew you," I said.

"Yeah," he snorted. "I thought I knew you too."

I saw a flicker of movement cross Lloyd's face like a frown. The boy's eyes opened, uncomprehending. He threw up his hands to push us away and hurled himself over the edge of the bed of the truck and fell into the snowbank. He looked around, pulled himself to his knees and stumbled across the road. He fell as he hit the hard snowbank on the other side, then scrambled up. I noticed then there was a break in the dense black tamaracks. He fell face forward and gave a shriek, disappearing on the other side of the snowbank. He was lost in the falling snow.

"Let him go. Let him go," Brett screamed at me. He grabbed me by the sleeve of my parka. I shrugged him off, not really understanding why. Who was this kid to me? I had walked by kids like him too many times and not seen.

I was across the road before I knew it and hit the snowbank running and flinging myself up and over. Ahead of me I could see Lloyd's floundering progress, the places where he'd run a few steps, fallen and got up again.

Brett was behind me. "Wait. Wait."

The trees thinned out and a clearing opened. Ahead was an old log cabin, built low, the snow piled up to the windows. Power lines strung in from the road dipped low under a burden of ice. It was so cold that smoke from the chimney went straight up. A snow machine and an old truck were hummocked with snow. The woodpile set under an overhang stayed dry. A light shone in one window.

Lloyd had floundered his way across the clearing, up the flagstone steps and disappeared inside.

You just don't barge up to people's houses way back here. Lloyd knew we were there. We stood waiting, stamping our boots to stay warm. Minutes passed. Then an old woman stood on the porch, long skirt, boots, scarves, toque, a rifle pointed down.

"You people leave him alone," she shouted.

"We were trying to help him, you old hag," Brett shouted back at her, his voice thick with anger.

"We just want to know Lloyd's okay," I said, stepping forward. "Is he okay?"

The rifle came up an inch or two, then the stumpy old woman turned away and slammed the door.

"Let's go," Brett said. "What are you waiting for? They don't want us here."

I knew that. What was I waiting for, my lungs hurting, toes freezing? I didn't want to get back in the truck with Brett. I didn't want to go back to living in Dad's basement with him. My Dad called him *that guy* and wouldn't look at him.

I wanted to fight. I wanted to blow the whole thing up. He could go back to LA where everything was apparently better. I could get a job and do hard-time living with my Dad, listen to *Family Feud* booming through the floorboards into my basement room. I could do it. Everything that held Brett and me together was easily detached.

I had walked past kids like Lloyd too many times. I had walked straight into it with Brett. Straight into him, dazzled. Two months of high summer on the beach and I'd brought him home, promising him adventure.

We just had to get through Hearst, Kapuskasing, Cochrane, Timmins. Maybe I could put him on the train there. Let him wait for the train outside on the platform in the freezing cold.

Mar Preston is the author of six semi-hardboiled crime fiction novels set in Los Angeles and a tranquil California mountain town, and an e-Book series titled *Writing Your First Mystery*. She returned to Ottawa in 2019 after a 50-year hiatus in California, and has been surprised to find she can almost *enjoy* the Canadian winter.

Judge's Comment

A story focused on the narrator realizing both her partner's failing and her own. Utterly lacking in compassion, her partner is exposed as a racist and selfish fool. But the narrator is forced to confront her own indifference and ignorance after a shocking turn of events, and how her own choices led her to this moment. The author notes the turning point of her narrator in the finale as she must change her life in response. I liked that the writer was forcing the reader to confront the uncomfortable.

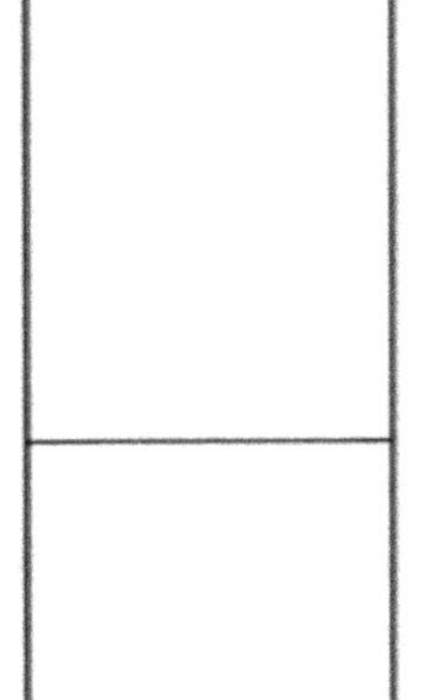

HONOURABLE MENTION

ANNA RUMIN

CROSSING DECEPTION PASS

I've been watching her all night — it was her shin that caught my eye, long and thin and smooth; so familiar. They're all the same — the winter doesn't bother them or their exposed lean limbs whose only consent to the cold are the small goosebumps I can almost feel from my sentry post. Older, more experienced, more practical women are bundled up and trudge a few steps behind, muttering how foolish the younger ones are, forgetting or perhaps not wanting to remember that they too once strode through the world with bare legs and arms and heads even in the winter, although never in the rain. I've seen them all; I've hunted many and enjoyed more than my share. They forget that if they scream it makes matters worse; they forget that their backs are invitations, that the smallest amount of almond or lemon or vanilla-scented body-cream is a summons. This new one glows, and my mouth is moist at simple possibility.

Alicia. This is what I will call her. Alicia has arrived with a friend whose shins aren't quite as long, hair quite as glossy, skin quite as polished. Alicia is ever so slightly slumped and only looks up when she laughs which is often but not so often, so that most of the time she is looking at the ground. Every once in a while, she bumps into her friend. Alicia's is a crooked walk, and charming in a crooked kind of way. They giggle and sing and laugh oblivious to the night around them, drunk on whatever the bartender indulged them with, loudly recounting the conversation they had with a wealthy hair-dresser and his pet poodle, lamenting that the dreamy piano-player never once looked up from the keys. And, from only one night of observation, Alicia and her friend going back and forth from the chalet to the lodge, I can already tell that she is a screamer, that she will turn her back and run leaving the scent of vanilla cream that will be my guide.

On the second day she is with her family, bundled and ready for the winter that nestles into the mountains and stays and grows and only leaves when the bears begin to stir, their stomachs empty and waiting to be filled with what the sun has begun to nourish. Even in her indigo-blue winter gear she is divine and I imagine her hair tumbling out when she removes her shiny white helmet. She is arguing with her family or rather they are all arguing. I can hear the complaints, the same ones I have grown used to hearing all these years: *Nobody listens to me! Why is it so dark when it is supposed to be morning in the Rockies? This is so stupid why are we even leaving?* Why indeed? She isn't used to seeing in the dark, she isn't used to a moon and stars that light up a sky, she isn't used to greeting the daylight with gratitude. Her every move is so predictable that I sit back and yawn. I might as well take a nap until I see her again in the evening when she will bare her legs and strut down the snowy road with her confident friend in search of excitement at the lodge. I will be there watching; but like all the others before her, she won't know.

The next morning I see Alicia again, in the dark, this time quiet, and I follow her little family. They've got packs on their backs and one by one they begin to ski into the backwoods far away from the chalet, from the road, from the lodge. At first, it is easy; the sun comes out and I can see she has no idea what is in store for her after this first wooded area. She stops, her brother stops, and they laugh and pull out a bag of nuts and a bottle of water and exchange stories and laugh some more. I see what could be their fatal mistake — earphones. And they

Anna Rumin is a native Montrealer whose identity has been shaped by her home province, her Russian roots, a passion for life-long learning that has been woven both formally in academia both at home and internationally and informally through travel, voracious reading and writing, the belief that each person has a unique story to tell, and a near obsession with the outdoors. She designs and teaches memoir-based writing courses and in her spare time she enjoys feeding friends and family, painting, playing in the Gatineau, and writing short fiction.

continue their journey, singing loudly, oblivious to the sounds they cannot hear all round them. And I follow, not so quietly anymore because really, I don't need to. Branches break, and when I stop to shit, even then the smell does not deter them so I don't bother to cover it up like I normally do.

It is a long journey for this family of four. They think they are fit, like all the others who come here in their red, orange and blue Gore-Tex. When the woods end and the wind begins, they recognize that their journey has changed. Alicia falls behind her family and stops to breathe and drink and stupidly eat more nuts, which results in her hands getting cold. It is at that moment I first hear her sweet whimper and know that it won't be long before someone in her pack turns, sees she is out of view, and skis back toward her. Her father does so and goes behind her as if this will make her work harder, go faster and complain less when all Alicia wants, and this I know from all the others, is to be sitting at the lodge, her bare legs crossed and her hands caressing a glass of something that sparkles amongst others who hold similar glasses and who, unlike me, pretend to ignore her shins.

Once they are through the first pass they will need to cross a lake. It is here the wind picks up and tries its best to push them back, to keep them from crossing, from getting to the next and most difficult pass. I stay behind — I know this route well, I've done it many, many times. I remember back to the first time when I thought I had lost my mother, and then I thought I was lost when she reappeared and reassured me that I would never be alone, that I needed to trust my instincts. This family is tougher than I thought and sooner than I thought they have crossed and are ready for the hardest pass. The first climb is long and Alicia has slowed down and eventually, as I knew she would, she stops to rest. Her cheeks are pink, her eyes glow and I see little clouds of breath going in and out of her mouth — the quarter and half-notes of her soul. Her father stays and then they begin to climb again reaching the first plateau framed by the peaks of these western mountains where I live, that I love, that I know. The wind forces even me to squint and I know this next part, the deceptive part, will be the hardest. But they push forward and soon they are at the second summit and they stop to take photos, to document their nearly achieved goal in harsh conditions that only the Rockies know how to deliver. And I am moved by Alicia's silence as she gazes at the mountains before her.

The last few kilometres are a downhill gift and soon they arrive at the tiny cabin that will be their home for the next two nights. They don't know that they will grow to love this place like I do — even if I can only peer in through the windows and watch them cuddled on couches, playing guitar or sitting at the candle-lit table. But I don't mind, I have my own space to rest and think and plan. I do my best not to think too much, not to let myself wander back to that place where I will find my mother's body covered in blood. I won't let myself go to that day when one moment we were alive, whistling, purring, yawning and the next she was dead and nothing I could do would bring her back. They took her body away before I could honour her or say goodbye — her legs dragging and scraping the ground before they flung her onto the sled and sped away leaving me behind, not even knowing that I was there. I lay in the spot where she fell and then covered it up. I close my eyes, curl myself against the tree and fall asleep under these boughs.

I watch Alicia for two days. She is quiet but not unhappy, I think. I see her under blankets reading, playing cards with her brother and drinking cups of tea. She doesn't change clothes for two days; there is no running water or electricity and Alicia ties her hair in a ponytail, puts ChapStick on her lips and eats cookies the way she used to when she was a little girl. Once a day she ventures outside and skis with her family. She is prettiest when she falls in the snow — her eyelashes and hair covered in white, her cheeks bright red, her laughter filling the air with the notes from the winter birds. After she is up and continues on her route, I lie down in the nest her body has made and breathe in the scent of her, feel her warmth and hear her laughter.

The day they leave it will snow more than it ever has, ever, ever. It will begin just as the sun goes down and it will continue, beautiful at first, flakes so big she will want to save and draw them. They will marvel at their luck, at being in the mountains when it snows, but when it doesn't stop and when the mountain tops begin to rebel, heave and finally purge their sides of snow boulders, when they feel the avalanches first in their feet then in their stomachs and still hear them long after they have stopped, then this little family will quietly, respectfully and with reverence, grow just a little scared. Fear, as I have found, is a good thing.

It is the brother who leads, one heavy step after the other breaking through the snow that now goes up to his thigh. He is strong, just like my brother, made for the mountains. Alicia stays behind and I can feel her tension as strongly as I can feel the muscles in my back. She follows her brother and her mother follows her and her father follows the mother and I follow them all. The pace is excruciating as they climb the hill that only two days earlier they flew down. When they are at the top they remember why it is called Deception Pass; as soon as they descend they must summit the first and then second, hidden pass. I can hear them inhale, exhale, inhale, exhale. Alicia yells, *Fuck the Rockies*! But she has no choice, she has to carry on.

Between avalanches, in the wind and snow, the others follow the brother step by step by step until they are up and over the first pass, and then the second, and then they are crossing the lake, and then the final pass until they are at the woods where the wind has stopped, where there is no sign of falling snow, where the sun warms their faces and hearts. They stop, and take photos and laugh and eat and are on their way again. The brother is way ahead followed by the father who is whistling. And then I hear Alicia's mother whistle and I remember my own mother's chirping.

Alicia falls behind, puts her earphones in, and begins to ski in the trail her brother has made. She is the girl I remember from a few days ago — arrogant and confident and wilful. I hear her sing and follow the string of notes.

And now I am ready.

I've done this so many times that I don't bother to think before my chase and just as I get close enough, Alicia stops, turns around, and sees me. And for whatever reason, I stop too. Alicia doesn't scream, she doesn't turn her back on me, and the wind that died down doesn't carry that warm vanilla scent I know is hers. I stare at her blueberry eyes, her rose-bud mouth and the little nibbly earlobes from which now dangle her white earphones. She is still singing softly when she stops, stares at me, straightens her spine, and whispers, *leave me alone*. I watch a stain between her legs grow bigger, I smell the sweat that I know is pooling under her arms, I feel her body tremble, but still she stands and stares into my eyes and repeats, *leave me alone*. And she doesn't scream.

My mother screamed, not when she was killed, she didn't have time to. She screamed when she was alive. But mostly, my mother chirped when she couldn't find me and I would chirp back and then we'd be together until we weren't. Alicia is alone now — her father and brother and mother are so far ahead that even if she called out they'd never ever have time to come back. And when they do finally realize she's missing, they'll find the stains and the brief remains, more than what was left for me. And they will lie down in the spot like I did, they will be changed forever, their little family even smaller, and much, much quieter.

Leave me alone.

And I do.

Long after she thought I was gone, long after I had slowly retreated when I heard the others coming, I watched her begin to cry, eventually sobbing so hard I thought she might break. I watched until she stopped, turning her back to me and to the mountains, and began skiing to where she knew her family waited for her, digging out the car that would take them back to the lodge where she would tell the story of crossing Deception Pass where she met me, and stood her ground, and I let her go.

Judge's Comment

The story begins quietly, a slow pacing marked by the eyes narrating the story. There is a quiet reserve here. Observed from afar, the child that the (non-human) narrator stalks becomes a lens for the uncertainties and cruelties experienced by her pursuer. Moving.

FINALIST

H. A. EILANDER

MOCK ME, MAKE ME

I keep waking up to drawn curtains and car alarms. Every hour I stir just to hear those short bursts rage on and on, as I let my bruises steep in the darkness so I can't see their colours change. And when my parents knock on my door with their deepest concerns creased in their foreheads, I let them know that I'm in pain.

It's a migraine, I lie. They've already decided that my other ailment must be in my head.

Why do you want this kind of attention? This is a nice neighbourhood, they said, as if "nice" meant the same as "good".

The car alarm starts again.

Jesus, I hear my mother mutter through the door. *She gets those migraines from your side of the family, you know.*

My father disagrees. It's her side that passes down all the head issues. Neither knows their bickering is irrelevant.

I roll away from the crack of light searing through a space between the curtains and squeeze my earplugs into my ear canals as deep as they will go. It works until it doesn't. They, inevitably, always fall out.

***

Snow White and Cinderella's fates were sealed with songbirds, unbreakable glass, and long lasting first kisses. They were romanced and given happily ever afters with their princes, and I have never in my life wanted to be less like them.

***

The knock on the door felt like a knock on my bones. With my parents out, I peered from my door frame to the shadow at the front of the house, the officer's silhouette fracturing into inkblots through the frosted geometric designs of the door's glass.

An angel. A bird. A reaper.

I didn't want to answer, but he called when he caught my movement.

Your neighbour's car was broken into last night, said the tall man in black and blue. His colours were stitched, while mine were finger-painted on. He asked me if I had heard or seen anything.

I nodded and told him about the car alarms and he asked me when.

All day, I said, my insides shaking and my outsides stiff. *All day, since late last night.*

Now he nodded, but he looked disappointed when he asked, *Are you sure you didn't notice anything else?*

Was anything taken?

No.

Wrong, I thought.

Just vandalized, he said, staring at me, unblinking.

Just.

But we still take it very seriously.

It was difficult not to look away, but I managed and asked, *Has anybody seen anything?*

Listen, miss, I know you recently filed a complaint against your neighbour.

No, I reported a crime.

And, unfortunately, we found no evidence. Can't destroy someone's life on hearsay.

It wasn't fear that caused my shaking then.

Have you found any witnesses to the vandalism, officer?

We're hoping one of the neighbours might have noticed something.

I hoped so too.

***

Didn't Snow White talk to birds? Sing to them? Until the glass coffin, at least. Once upon an enchanted death she couldn't sing anymore, or dance with the dwarves, but she could be kissed.

She was. Everyone saw it, witnessed the love and celebrated its truth, but I wonder if it would have still been romantic if it were just the prince and Snow White.

Because it could have been something else entirely.

***

I split the wall of curtain in two and exposed myself to the reality outside. Someone was tending to their lawn, a little boy chased his friend down the sun-splattered sidewalk, and a red car with a broken passenger window bared its glass fangs in my direction, daring me to approach it. If I stood too close it would bite me.

I could bite harder. I had already.

The car alarm blared loudly then, beating against its own echoes that had been imprinted on my eardrum since yesterday, but the headlights didn't flash now, and though I knew it couldn't be, I wondered if maybe it was all in my head.

There were no witnesses. Maybe there could be.

***

In an older version of *The Frog Prince*, the princess never kissed the frog. She said she would, but when that damn amphibian hopped to her castle and into her bed, she changed her mind.

But you promised, he said.

But you swore it, chided the king.

The princess wasn't perfect in any way, but she did stand her ground.

Get out of my bed, she screamed at the frog, and when he protested again, she threw him against the wall.

That's what ended the curse — a protest and violence, and that's when they knew she meant it. Poof! He was human. Poof! He was gone and they never saw each other again.

Some kisses are everything to a princess, but sometimes they're not. Sometimes it's nothing, and that's the everything she wants.

***

I didn't wait for it to grow dark this time. When I grabbed my baseball bat, I gave it a few practice swings and marched outside where the sun could glint off the metal. My parents looked at me, perplexed, as did a few of the neighbours, but even with the attention and the heat of the sun, the long shadow of the house next door made my skin prickle and wash over with ice.

Perhaps the damned toad was watching. His car was wailing again, and again the sound was disconnected from the vision before me. No headlights flashed and the alarm carried from elsewhere.

I ran up to it, looked around and upwards, and laughed, because a bird was singing to me and I understood every lyric. The alarm wasn't only in my head at all. Way, way up where the trees were practically sky, a mockingbird clung to the branches there, its song a scream.

And I loved it, because it was music to me.

I walked around to the driver's door, and ratta-tap-tapped on the glass, lightly with my fingernails. Then I knocked it hard like I'd been knocked, and smacked it till it stung my palm red, but it would not break. When I raised my bat high, the mockingbird let the world know there were predators about with her siren and the puffing of feathers, bright as snow and dark as cinders.

When the spiderwebs appeared in the glass after the first hit, I remembered when my kicking foot had done nothing at all. When the car rallied with birdsong, I felt when my voice was smothered by a lack of evidence, a lack of witnesses. And when the bat swung a heavy hitter and broke his world into shards, I could only hear the sweet nothings that cursed my ears — *my angel, my princess, my beauty, my love* — and feel the heavy weight that pressed against my body and pushed my angel wings down, down, twisting tighter and tighter, until they, too, broke beneath my shattering.

I swung and smashed and bent and broke the unholiest of bodies. The car and the bird and I all screamed as it warped, and she and I cursed it all. The glass wouldn't be unbreakable anymore. I wouldn't be some gentle princess with a bird who mocked me, her song a scream, and I'd be able to hear the real sirens, because there'd be evidence now and witnesses too.

I breathed long and slow, grasping the bat. Above me, the bird with feathers of snow and ash silenced her song and eyed my red, shattered coffin below. The branches of her tree were a broken cage against sky, and beneath the heavens I set us angels free.

Contented, I sighed. Happily, I lived.

H. A. Eilander splits her time between managing a food shop out in the country, playing the violin, and cuddling with her two Scottish terriers. She has previously been published in the speculative fiction anthology *Making Monsters* and has a master's degree in English Language and Literature from the University of Waterloo, which was spurred on by her fascination with monsters, both mythical and human.

Judge's Comment

What drew me to the story wasn't the overall narrative but the way the author plays with interleaving fairy-tale mythology within the storylines. The clever interplay of the expected and unexpected and ultimately, the protagonist's capacity to twist the fairy tale's happily ever after into something more earned than granted.

FINALIST

P. R. ISFELD

LITTLE THINGS

The bee darts in through a crack in the window frame, seeking warmth as summer slips into September. She heads toward Derek's bouquet of overblown roses, buzzes around my face, then approaches my blinking eye, and flies back to the window. I hear her banging against the screen, terrified, desperate to escape into the dawning sun. Trapped. I'd be pounding against that window too, if my muscles obeyed me.

One of us will die in this antiseptic little room. It's just a question of who goes first. And who casts the death blow.

If only that orderly would open the goddam screen.

***

The Count came again last night, even as the night nurse's footsteps receded down the corridor toward the geriatric wing. He's not really a Count, of course, but he has an aristocratic, slightly creepy demeanour. Back in the day, as one of Ottawa's most powerful civil service mandarins, he cast an evil power over all the women who stumbled into his orbit. If you needed your job you feared him.

The Dracula thing was a joke, or so we told ourselves. Like whistling past a graveyard. It wasn't that funny then and it's not funny now. Napoleon Syndrome, even in old age. I escaped his clutches when I worked in his department. Now I'm trapped.

The old bastard's putrid breath assaulted my nostrils before he spoke. "Wake up, honey." His fingers slid down my arm like snakes, then plucked the call button from my cramped hand. It hurt.

"I know you're awake, don't pretend." He reached across the railing of my bed and turned my head to face him. I could just make out his face, the widow's peak still his most distinguishing feature, even at his age. The asshole must be pushing eighty. And he's in better shape than I am, despite the thirty-odd years between us.

That doesn't take much.

Thank goddess he moved his hands before my tears reached them. Female distress is like Viagra to this monster.

Small victories.

"Such a shame about you," he crooned. "Such a blow to your pride."

It was a virus, you ass. Guillain Barré syndrome can happen to anyone.

"Then that lover of yours. All those bouquets, but none of the man himself. A bit like my own family, really." He paused. "At least you're giving me the deference I deserve."

He brushed the hair from my forehead and brought his wizened lips close to mine.

Don't gag.

"Let me tell you a story."

I tell myself again that it's a dream. It doesn't work this time.

***

Harsh clanging. Soft voices. Apologies.

The new girl must have opened the wrong set of doors and set off the alarm. The old hands won't let this pass: five months of forced observation have taught me the nursing profession eats its young.

The new girl slides her tattooed forearms under my shoulders and sits me up, then settles herself onto the hard-backed chair beside me. She's strong but her caramel-coloured hand trembles as she picks up the plastic fork.

Don't worry, I rarely bite.

Alma, one of the lifers, appears in the doorframe. "Good morning, Karen. I see you've met Mandy," she says with a smile, then focuses on the aide. "You need to watch her face to see what she wants to eat. She'll smile or blink once for yes and twice for no. And go slowly, okay? This takes a lighter touch than security work."

The girl nods. She's young enough to be my daughter, if I had one.

I've never liked scrambled eggs, but Mandy is slow and careful, giving me time to chew and swallow, so I eat a few bites to show my appreciation. I do like the blueberries. She pops them into my mouth one by one, in a way that makes me think of Jake, my chihuahua. He loves eating berries like that.

"I hope I'm doing this right," Mandy says. "Let me know, huh?" I smile and move my chin up and down.

"It's only my second day," she continues. "I'm hoping you guys are easier to be around than the shoplifters I used to chase in my old job. Alma told me we don't have many patients here who get home, though. Everyone's cheering for you."

I blink as fast as I can. If I'm going to recover without years of rehabilitation, the first six months are crucial. We're on month five. I'm working hard, but some days ...

"Alma says they'll miss you," she said. "Everyone says you're one of our nicest patients."

I resist the urge to roll my eyes. Hard to be difficult when you can barely move. Impolitic, too, when you depend on the goodwill of the nurses. I hate how they talk about us, especially in front of other patients, but I can't let that show. They take better care of the happy ones.

Alma reappears just as Mandy wipes the last of the eggs from my chin. "Mandy, I need you to come and help me with something as soon as you're finished. Odds are we won't deal with this again for a while, but you might as well get used to it up front. They need help on the geriatric side often enough."

Mandy gets up, flashing a nervous smile. "Let me open the window and let that bee out first," she says. "We wouldn't want the poor thing to sting someone."

Alma nods without looking my way. "I'm afraid it will be a little longer than usual before Mandy gets back for your physio."

She turns the TV to the weather channel and closes the door.

Hmmm. The privacy of a closed door is a rare thing here. When the gurney rattles by half an hour later, I know. I can't see the parking lot from my bed, but I'm sure the coroner's van is there.

That afternoon the attendants huddle in the hallway, muttering about poor Emily from the nursing home, and the bruising on her thighs when they found her.

The Count told me the truth.

At least the bee escaped.

***

"You need to rest, that's all," Derek had said, stroking my hair back from my forehead, just before he left me in that greyish winter dawn. He and I met at the Westin for a naughty lunch once a month. I loved the illicit escapism of it all, even though the hotel was only a few blocks from both my condo and his office on the Hill.

"I think I need an ambulance," I moaned, but he shook his head.

"You've just got the flu," he said, backing out the door. "Checkout's not until 1100, that's nearly five hours. You'll be fine after some sleep."

At least housekeeping found me in time to call 911. The paramedics got me to the hospital and onto a respirator quickly enough to save my life. In the old days, I would have been strapped into an iron lung.

Now Derek has vanished from my life like a ghost, his only trace a rotting bouquet of roses and a card with "to the strongest woman I know" written in a neat florist's hand. His weakness is understandable, really. The wife could ruin his career and his life if she ever found out.

Time to let it — and him — go.

But now I must fight the old man alone.

***

The Count lets me sleep through the night after Emily's death.

The next, he jolts me awake with a greasy paw on my forehead. Disgusting. But maybe he's sick. I can only hope.

"We haven't discussed what does it for me. Have we?"

I stare straight ahead, unblinking. Of all the rehab facilities in all the hospitals in this shit town, I have to land next to the geriatric unit that warehouses this old monster. Small world.

Small city, anyway.

My silence doesn't deter him. This isn't a conversation, any more than his infamous "performance discussions" with women used to be.

"You need to understand, don't you, darling?"

I am not your darling. And I will never understand.

"I used to practise the art of persuasion

on you ladies, and now I can simply take what I want. But Emily was too easy. There has to be a challenge. I need a spark."

He grabs my jaw and peers at me, as if to help me absorb the implications of this pronouncement.

"They don't notice my work in the other wing. Direct competition from the Grim Reaper himself."

A door slams at the end of the corridor and his grip on my chin constricts. It hurts, but I refuse to flinch.

"We're going to have to continue this tomorrow, my darling. It would cause quite the scandal if the orderly walked in on us."

He slinks back into the gloom. The attendant pauses outside my door but looks through me when I try to make eye contact.

Just like the old days.

***

One fall evening when I was seventeen, I went to the movies alone. As the opening credits rolled, a middle-aged man plunked himself beside me and slapped his paw on my thigh. My upper thigh. I froze for a moment, then the stench of stale cigarettes and beer hit my nose. I grabbed his hand and yelled "What is this doing on my leg?" He whimpered like a kicked dog and slunk off, followed by the guffaws of my seatmates.

The film vanished in a haze of adrenaline and pride. Afterwards, I strode through my front door, triumphant in victory, and told my mom how I had vanquished the monster.

Her sideways glance sliced into me like a knife.

"You disrupted people's movie over such a little thing?" she said. "A lady would have just moved."

"What about *my* movie?" I demanded, slamming the door to my room.

Silence. Of course.

The next day, a bruise bloomed on my thigh.

What would a "lady" do now, Mom?

***

Mandy raises my right leg and then lets it go, and I hold it up for a second before it falls onto the bed. She picks up the other one, and I show off by shifting it to the side a few inches. The small movements take all my strength and concentration, but I love seeing the big grin split the aide's round, open face.

She calls Alma, who rewards me with her own smile. "You're making real progress," she says, "but I wish we could get your speech back."

I move my lips in what I hope is a smile and blink as fast as I can. A bead of sweat slides between my eyebrows. *You and me both, lady.*

Something twitches in the doorframe behind Alma. The Count. Watching us. I close my eyes.

He underestimates me, and I need to keep it that way.

Mandy's voice is soothing, concerned. "You need to rest."

"Let's get you back to your ward, Mister MacDonald," says Alma, turning into the corridor. "They shouldn't be letting you roam around, especially not these days."

Mandy leans closer to me. "They all say he's harmless," she whispers, "but that old guy gives me the creeps. I know that type from way back."

I blink my eyes as fast as I can. *Me too.*

***

Derek's roses are long gone, replaced by a potted mum from my coworkers, and the bees are back. They beat against the screen from outside the window this time. Fall is here now, and they're fighting to get inside. Every so often one of them succeeds, only to die on the windowsill. Poor little things.

There's another sudden death in the geriatric ward. Attendants patrol the corridors more often. Mandy comes in for extra night shifts and she stops by to do a few extra exercises with me whenever she can.

My vocal chords start to work again, but I can't yet form an intelligible word. The days pass in a blur of physio and speech therapy that leaves me exhausted, sliding into heavy sleep. I don't have much control over my fingers, but in my dreams, I can sit up again.

The Count stays away for two weeks, and I start to hope that he's dead.

But inevitably, the night after my neighbour brings me Hallowe'en photos of Jake in his tiny vampire costume, I awake to the rasp of desiccated lips against my forehead. I turn my head and he grabs my chin with his dry claws, yanking my face toward him.

I close my eyes and he slaps my cheek hard enough to sting.

Silently, I curse the arrogance that led me to drop the call button on the nightstand beside me, rather than on the bed like previous nights.

He knows I almost laughed today.

"You always were a passive-aggressive little bitch," he growls, his face red in the dim light of the tv console. "But it's hard to be aggressive these days, isn't it?"

Aggressive is the easy part. I force myself to stay motionless.

He's still holding my jaw with one hand, as the other slithers over my breast, dragging the covers with it. He climbs onto the bed and jams his knee between mine, letting go of my face to steady himself with his hands on my hips.

"I'm going to enjoy you even more than the others," he whispers. "Emily will be tough to beat. She wept so prettily."

I don't weep.

"You think you're not going to cry, but you're wrong." He moves one hand toward the pocket of his pyjamas and pulls out a comb, the old-fashioned kind, with a pointy handle. "In the old days, I preferred knife-play — fully consensual of course — but in reduced circumstances, one must make do."

I swallow.

Deep breath. Eyes on the prize.

He claws at my nightgown with his free hand, dragging the hem up my thighs.

My blood thrums in my ears.

Now.

"Mandy!" I scream, sitting up and raising my knee as hard as I can and knocking him sideways.

He bounces off the windowsill and hits the floor and his howl brings the nurse's aide through the door.

Later on, when I'm able to talk to the police, I tell them how he thrashed around, banging his head on the floor. My story matches Mandy's.

Maybe it was some kind of epileptic fit. They happen in people that age, especially under stress from something like a bee sting.

Those little things can cause such trouble.

P. R. Isfeld has spent more than twenty years in the federal government, seeking refuge from bureaucracy by writing fiction. Although she moved to the National Capital Region toward the end of the last century, she has never lost her love of the CB radios and long road-trips that were part of her prairie childhood.

Judge's Comment

A deeply disturbing story that borders on a thriller. Almost Hitchcock-like in its mood and temperament, the story builds until the breaking point. I appreciated the story's focus on an autonomy grounded beyond the body. A stubborn resilience and point of resistance.

FINALIST

PAM MADDIN-BAKER

BASTA

Waking from a troubled dream, Elisa tightened her arms around her five-year-old son, Diego. She breathed in the fresh, chilly air. Even in tropical Mexico, the highlands were frosty in midwinter. She wished she could stay beneath the wool coverlet with her boy. With a sigh, she rose and tucked the blanket around him.

Light from the full moon filtered in through gaps in the plank walls. She was puzzled by the quiet. Often after a New Year's Eve festival, men would still be up drinking. Shivering, she knelt to light a fire in the small stove in the middle of the hut to prepare breakfast before waking Diego.

Within minutes, the oak kindling crackled and smoked. She hated the smoke from the uncovered stove. It stung her eyes. With skilled hands, she formed a few small tortillas from their last bit of ground maize. These were needed to keep Diego's stomach quiet for their long walk to the market this morning.

A full pot of water was ready to be warmed on the stove. Yesterday, she had hauled a heavy jug up the steep hill from the stream below the village. Now, it would be boiled for tea, but she would also use it for washing their hands and faces. Elisa could not forget the shame she felt once as a young child, when a light-skinned man had kicked her off a sidewalk in the city. He had called her a "dirty Indian". The words had stung more than the kick. The deeper meaning of the words is now clear to her. However, she would do what she could to protect Diego from such comments.

The scent of the cooking tortillas pulled her boy from sleep. He rubbed his eyes, sat up and looked around. "Mama, why is it dark? Is it a new year yet?"

"Yes," she smiled with love. "It is! A new year with new hopes! But it is very early," she added, handing him two warm tortillas, "and the sun will not be up for hours."

Chewing eagerly, he chattered at her between bites. "What year is it now, Mama? Was there a party last night? Did you see any fireworks?"

That fast talk reminded her of his father, Édouardo. With that snub nose and one drooping eyelid, he was the image of his papa. Elisa sighed and did her best to answer. "It is 1994. There was a small party, some dancing. You know I did not go! I was content to stay here with you."

Excited, he rushed on, "Will there be a party in the city today? Will there be firecrackers banging?"

His mother tried to keep answering, but her thoughts drifted off. Yesterday, Jorge (a middle-aged, plump man who had been watching her too carefully the past few weeks), had asked her to go with him to a fiesta in the village. Politely, she had said no, explaining she would need to put her child to bed early. But he had pressed, saying it was important to respect the rituals that marked the welcoming of a new year. She told him she would observe the rituals on her own. He had shrugged as if she was making a bad choice. But he did not ask again.

So at sunset, she had knelt alone before the small prayer table in her home, lit a long taper and prayed for the soul of her husband, Édouardo. Then, she and Diego snuggled on the straw mat, wrapped in the warmth of each other. She had worried they would be awakened by sounds of drunken men who would be drinking pox, a cheap alcohol. Often women and children

Pam Maddin Baker has always loved reading good stories. She studied Theatre Arts and English Literature at Ottawa University, and followed up by teaching those subjects for many years. When she retired, she found she had time to write her own stories! Since then she has been published online in Story Quilt, Canadian Stories, and WOW! Women on Writing.

would have to hide in the woods on these nights. She fell asleep thinking of how different things would be if Édouardo were still here; he was not like so many of the other village men. He did not drink and was never violent.

As she had drifted off to sleep, memories took control of her dreams. She imagined she was pleading again with Édouardo, *"Do not confront them. They will kill you."*

He answered her, *"It isn't fair, they did not pay me."*

Then, still in the dream, she was wandering through the mist of the mountains, calling his name. Like ghosts in the fog, policemen floated around her, smoking fat cigars. They sneered, *"Go home. He is probably drunk and sleeping in a ditch."*

The nightmare was always the same. It always ended with her searching and searching the jungle.

Diego's little voice broke into her thoughts. "When are you going to eat, Mama?" He had almost finished his food.

"I am not hungry yet." She winked to assure him. "I will wait until we get to the city." He gave her a look of doubt, tore the warm bread in two and handed her the larger piece. She gave up and accepted his kindness.

A few minutes later they stood outside their home, hand-in-hand ready for the journey to the city of San Cristóbal. Elisa wore a black wool skirt and a cotton blouse with intricate embroidery of red and black across the front which proudly represented her Tzotzil heritage. A warm shawl hugged her shoulders. Two long braids of coal-black hair trailed down her back, the ends neatly tied together with ribbon. This was how her ancestors had worn their hair many centuries ago and today the style remained unchanged. Diego wore a warm sweater with some small holes and blue jeans. Both of them were barefooted.

Elisa scanned the village lit by moonlight. Tin roofs topped wooden shacks. Garbage lined dirt paths. Even the trees in the surrounding forests seemed to slump with despair. A stray dog curled up against a fence made from rusty bed springs. He raised his head to check them, but decided they were unimportant and tucked back to sleep.

Again, the unusual quiet in the village felt strange. The only sound was the scratching of a cat hunting for rats in a nearby alley. Foreboding entered Elisa like a creeping spirit. She forced herself to be brave. She and Diego had a difficult trip to make. They needed to start on the dirt trail that wound down the mountainside before sunrise. Only after walking for hours would they reach the tourist market and Diego would be exhausted by the time they arrived.

"Well, are you ready to see Jovel?" She used the Mayan name for the city. It meant "place in the clouds".

"Yes!" He gave a little hop, excited for his first visit to the city.

With a squeeze of his hand she set a quick pace. She did not want him to run ahead or dawdle behind, playing with sticks. In daylight, the switchback trails to the valley below were populated with travellers. But in these predawn hours, they could be dangerous and unpredictable.

Diego's stomach would begin to grumble before they arrived. But until his mother sold her embroidery work, they had no way to buy food. Elisa thought of the many long days of sitting on the ground sewing. She had decorated several yards of fabric with bright flower patterns to make table napkins. Great care was needed to keep the cloth from being stained by the constant dust. Hopefully the tourists would appreciate their value. She would sit outside the cathedral on the stone steps to try to sell them. Diego would sit beside her; his feet would hurt too much to play. She knew this from the times when she accompanied her mother to the city as a child.

Most of the village women bought and sold in the local market in Chenalhó on Saturdays. They avoided the city because of the piteous looks people would give them — as though they were beggars. But Elisa had no choice. With no food left and her neighbours having nothing to spare, she needed money now.

Hours later, sunlight was just creeping over the mountains when mother and child saw the first outlines of city buildings. Diego began to skip a little as they started down a narrow sidewalk tracing a cobblestone street. Wrought iron balconies hung with bougainvillaea flowers and festive decorations for the holiday season. The bright red, green and yellow picado banners cheered on the morning sun as it rose. The shops and homes began to warm in the morning glow.

Yet, Elisa felt an eerie stillness to the place. Where were the tourists? The shop owners? The delivery trucks? Her eyes scanned the street. A block ahead, half hidden behind trees, she spied two men in green uniforms. They were carrying rifles. Like a hare that freezes when it senses danger, she stopped. Her muscles tensed. She heard the rumbling of a low flying plane before she saw the Air Force bomber.

Diego tugged her to keep moving. "No, Diego," she whispered. "Stop! Look up at the plane."

He squinted up into the bright blue sky, searching above the red clay rooftops of the buildings. When he spotted the plane cruising in slow circles, his face lit up. "Mama! Will we see the plane land?"

She did her best to soften her face and knelt beside him. "I don't think so, Diego. Those are soldiers up there. I think we must go back home."

Tears started in his soft brown eyes as his bottom lip began to quiver. This was hard for him to understand. "But Mama we have walked so far!"

How could she explain to him what she feared? The past months there had been rumours in the village of a rebellion. She did not like thoughts of fighting and, despite the suffering she had been through, she could not join her people in this. Father Salvatore said violence was never the way to change men's hearts.

Torn between leaving and wanting to feed her son, she hesitated. "We will go a bit farther and see what is happening. But, Diego, you must listen to me. If I say it is time to go, we must turn around. Do you understand?"

He nodded his promise. They walked with caution, keeping close to the pastel walls of the houses. Only a few steps and a blast that felt like knives plunged into her ears. Elisa fell to her knees. A second later, thick whitish smoke filled the air around her. Trying not to inhale, she felt frantically around the space for her son.

Feeling his head, she crawled over and covered him with her body. Seconds passed. Gunfire peppered close by. A man screamed in pain. She scanned the area and saw a narrow alley between the storefronts. A jumbled stack of boxes there could hide them. She sprang up, grabbed her son and darted for cover.

Collapsing in the darkened alley, she squeezed her eyes shut and recited a prayer in Tzotzil, "Kuxetuk avo'on Maria ..."

Heavy boots pounded the pavement. Someone was running toward them. Glancing up, she saw two men in rough clothing and rubber boots stagger through the swirls of dust, one supporting the other. Their faces were covered with bandannas, but her eyes were drawn to the trail of blood that streaked the street behind them. The slumped man had a massive gash in his arm. It hung at a strange angle.

Elisa pushed aside her fear, and warned Diego not to move. She dashed out to help the two men. Grabbing the injured one around the waist, she helped haul him into the shelter of the alley. A space was cleared on the littered ground for him to lie down. Diego gawked at the spurting blood.

"Turn your eyes!" Elisa told him. He continued to stare. So, she directed him. "Go into my bag and take out my sewing." He handed her the stash of fine embroidered cloths. Her hands shaking, she pressed them against the bloody wound.

"Thank you," the man's partner said. "He spoke her native language. "I am Juan. This is my brother. You must be an angel."

But Elisa turned with fury. "Why are you doing this? You do not belong here. Are you starting a war?"

Juan tried to argue, "*Ya basta!* We say enough is enough. We did not begin this. It began in the hearts of our people centuries ago. If we can't own our land ..." A gunshot echoed in the alley. His eyes grew wide and, for a frozen moment, locked with Elisa's. Then he crumpled to the ground, blood oozing from his stomach.

In horror, she looked up to see two soldiers, one pointing a rifle directly at her, eyes cold and full of hate. The one with the gun grinned. A sly grin. In Spanish, he mocked her. "*Hola madre. Eres también un zapatista?*" She understood he was asking if she was a rebel. In a panic, she shook her head. The soldier ignored her and turned his aim at Diego. The gun blasted. The bullet narrowly missed, but broke off stucco from the wall behind them. Elisa howled in anguish. And the soldier laughed.

"*Vamanos!*" the other soldier yelled when they all heard a distant explosion. He shoved his partner to make him move and they were gone.

Elisa fell to her knees and hugged Diego to her chest, tears rolling down her cheeks. She heard a groan from Juan and crawled to his side. Refusing to let go of her son, she leaned over and heard Juan whisper, "Help ..."

"Yes," she answered, and removed the bandanna from the man's face, crushing it into a bandage to fit the wound in his stomach.

"No. Help you." With a weak gesture, he pointed to the pocket of his shirt. Elisa gently opened the button and pulled out a handful of pesos. Enough for a month's worth of food.

"No," she began.

He shook his head, looked at Diego, and then whispered, "Go now." He closed his eyes. Elisa said a prayer for him. She knew she could do nothing more for the brothers.

The sun was high in the noon sky, warmly toasting the pine and oak forest surrounding San Cristóbal as Elisa and Diego slipped back into the wilderness. The first day of the new year had unfolded with violence and bloodshed. Instead of firecrackers, Diego had heard gunfire. As they began their trek home, Elisa wrapped her knitted shawl around her blouse and skirt to cover the bloodstains from the day's violence. Yet, despite the sights her son had witnessed today, a new hope had begun to burn in her. The mountain her people needed to climb to fight for their dignity was as high and steep as the one she and Diego needed to climb to get home. But today they began to fight back. And she had stood with them.

Judge's Comment

A descriptive story set in a war zone. I enjoyed this story's focus on the particulars of the mother–son relationship and the intimate experience of the story. It ends with a shift in perspective, a re-accounting of one's personal position within the political but it's the intimate details that impressed me.

?

FINALIST

BARBARA WACKERLE BAKER

Barbara Wackerle Baker
grew up in Banff, Alberta. She loves writing, photography, exploring landscapes and time with grandchildren. Carousel Pictures made a mini film of her Globe and Mail essay, "Life Support", which played in the Toronto International Film Festival (fall 2019). Many of her short stories are in *Our Canada — Reader's Digest Magazine*, *Prairie Fire*, *The Globe and Mail*, *Chicken Soup*, and numerous anthologies.

THROUGH SHENA'S EYES

My people leave me again.

"It's just for a few hours," Kirsten says. She's the one with the dark hair and small hands. She kneels on the ground, wraps her arms around my neck and sticks her nose into my fur. "We'll be back soon, Shena."

I'm not sure why she calls me Shena. My name is Husky, descendant of the wolf family. I look around to see if anyone heard. We huskies have an image to uphold and I won't have it ruined by her silliness.

When I turn my head away, Kirsten lets go and stands.

"She'll be fine, I guess." She looks over at the tall man she calls Clifton. "I don't think she cares when we leave."

Clifton drapes his arm over Kirsten's shoulder.

"She'll miss you, hon," he says. "She'll miss your treats."

My ears perk up.

"See." Clifton laughs, digs in his coat pocket and pulls out a few kibbles. He puts his palm out in front of me. "Yeah, you and your treats, hey Shena?"

I ignore the reference to Shena again and swipe my tongue across his hand to scoop up the treats. They're not my favourite salmon flavoured ones but they'll do. When I've licked the crumbs off his palm, I go back to the giant pine tree in the corner of the yard. A squirrel was up there this morning. His endless high-pitched chirp was an irrefutable irritation. I stare into the branches. A flick of his bushy tail gives him away. I sit. And wait.

"Bye Shena," Clifton says.

Kirsten pats my head. "You be good."

I stare up the tree.

My tolerance for them, and humans in general, is just that — tolerance. These two seem decent enough, but I won't let my guard down. Not this time. They drive away and leave me alone with the old woman they call Gramma.

Gramma's okay but I know I frighten her. Watch this. I peel my lips back and let out a low growl.

"Shena," Gramma says in her trying-to-be-an-Alpha-dog voice. She takes a step back and shakes her finger at me. "You stop that. Be nice."

I close my mouth, pull my lips tight and grin. See. I told you. I don't think I'll bite her though. She takes me on long walks. And I can tell Gramma *wants* to like me. She's just not sure how to go about it. When she runs her hand down my shaved back, she says things like, "Easy Shena, you're okay."

Let's stop here for a minute and discuss my shaved body. A shaved husky? What the hell?

All those mutts in Kennel Ville sure got a good laugh when I came back from the groomer. It was hard to march by them with my head high, thankful they hadn't shaved it. They were worried about infection in my sores. Nonsense. They would have healed. Sooner or later. They'd been there for years.

Those inbred mutts constantly gossiped about my appearance. Like they had nothing else in their miserable lives to yap about. Punks. Them and their incessant barking. Feces stench. Everywhere. And always. Mongrels in cages stacked on top of each other, sometimes three high. The memory of the place makes me stiffen my neck. It was hard to maintain a sense of dignity in that shit hole.

But enough of that. Back to my here and now story.

I have blue eyes and a great profile. As soon as my coat grows back, I'll be a magnificent representative of our breed once more.

The squirrel never does come down.

Gramma takes me for a walk along the pathway by the river. An eclectic assortment of scents surrounds the tree trunks. Small, fresh dirt mounds stick up above the trimmed grass. Ground squirrel activity. I sniff too long and Gramma tugs on my harness. I stiffen my stance and stick my head down a hole.

"Leave them alone, Shena," Gramma says. "Let's go."

I trot ahead and turn my head side to side to keep track of all the ground squirrels at once. The varmints disappear here, pop up there. Sometimes there are two, then just one, sometimes three. I'd like to eat a few, but Gramma tugs me back when I get too close.

She walks fast. And Gramma talks even when there's no one around. When she jogs, I tighten the tension on the leash, hold my head high and run into the wind.

Up ahead, a herding dog, a young one, moves toward us like a hyena. Gramma slows down and snugs me up close to her leg.

"Don't worry, he's just a pup. He likes to play," the owner calls out. "He's friendly."

"I don't know what this one will do." Gramma's fingers wrap around my collar. "She's not mine. I'm just dog-sitting."

The other dog growls and lunges at me. His owner struggles to pull him back.

I stare straight ahead and march on by with Gramma.

"I'm sorry, so sorry." The man tries to control his dog without getting tripped up in the leash. "He never does that. He's friendly."

"Really?" Gramma mutters. She scratches my head. "Good dog, Shena. Stupid shepherd. Stupid shepherd owner. Friendly my ass."

After our long walk and a nice nap, I resume my squirrel-watching pose. Kirsten and Clifton drive up. What a surprise! People usually don't come back for me. I let them pat my head a few times before I move to the other side of the tree.

***

As I rest in my sunny spot in the back yard, Clifton brushes me. He's careful not to press hard on the old sores. Warmth seeps through to my skin. My world is calm. Quiet.

But then I hear a *bang*. Far away. And another one. Louder. I struggle to make sense of it. A dream? Reality? Metal slams against metal. Like someone hammers on a kennel. My kennel. I wake up. Frantic. Feel a hand on my head. I spin. Lunge. And grab the hand. Bite down. Hard.

I realize too late. It's Clifton's hand.

Clifton doesn't say a word. His face scrunches up. I can't see his eyes. He pushes me down, presses his knee into my neck. Clamps fingers over my nostrils. When I gasp, he pulls his hand out.

What have I done?

Clifton and Kirsten don't get mad. They get sad. Kirsten cries. Often. She stares at me. Tears drip down her face. Clifton wraps his big arm around her and holds her close.

They make me wear a contraption on my snout. I wear it outside all the time. And even in the house if Kirsten is home alone. But I get used to it.

I'm just so thankful they don't send me back to Kennel Ville.

***

And then the day comes when they take me into a building. It smells of metal and death. I brace my front legs. Straight out.

Clifton clears his throat. "Come on, Shena."

Kirsten's small fingers stroke my head. I look up at her. Tears run down her face.

We follow a man into a room. My nostrils burn. The door closes. There is nowhere to go so I lean against Clifton's leg. The man in blue clothes talks in a quiet voice. Clifton tells me to lie down. He offers a salmon treat.

All three of them kneel beside me.

There's a poke in my hip. I don't mean to, but I whine. Something burns under my skin. Like a fire. But I can't see where the flame is. I try to ignore it as I munch the treat. And then another whine slips out. It gets hard to breathe. I can only pant. Short. Puffs.

I look at Clifton, at Kirsten and blink ... a lot. Fingers stroke my cheeks, my ears. Their voices muffle like they're far away, but they're right here, beside me. They never leave.

And then it gets quiet. And dark.

***

The full moon lights up the entire valley as I run beside the very river we walked by on my last day. I lick fresh salmon juice off my lips. My coat gleams. It's long and magnificent. My eyes pierce through the darkness and I howl. My howl vibrates and echoes through the night as it follows the wind. Surely you can hear me.

After miles of trotting through the forest my legs tire. I search for a hollow. Leaves crunch as I turn in circles to tramp them down. With a long sigh, I drop and curl my head into my shoulder. And sleep.

In my dream, I run hard and fast. And I howl. For you.

***

"Hey there," someone says. "Come here, pup."

I recognize the voice. My eyes blink the sleep away.

Where is my forest? My moon? The dark night?

"What if we call you Rizzo?" the familiar voice says.

I stare down at stubby, white paws. Brown and black lines run up short legs. I turn my head and see I have a puppy body covered in black and brown fur. Markings of a Bernese Mountain Dog. Where is my husky coat? My long, run-in-the-wind legs?

"Rizzo, I have a treat."

Fresh salmon smells reach my nostrils.

Who is this Rizzo she speaks of? I look around.

"Come here Rizzo."

When I stand up, my legs wobble. The salmon smell gets stronger. She can call me whatever she wants. I waddle over. Lick the treat out of her fingers. Her small hand rubs my head. I roll on my back. My little tail thumps of its own accord.

Judge's Comment

The central character in this story isn't human but her observations are humane. Marked by relative restraint and an attention to detail without falling into sappiness, the story pulses at its core with compassion.

ACKNOWLEDGEMENTS

Thanks to everybody who helped out with everything, especially during this difficult time dealing with COVID-19 adventures/challenges.

Special thanks always to the entrants. I know it sounds silly to say that without you we wouldn't have a contest, but think about it. We wouldn't.

Sherrill Wark
NCWC Coordinator

www.ingramcontent.com/pod-product-compliance
Lightning Source LLC
Chambersburg PA
CBHW080459030726
47592CB00011B/3183

* 9 7 8 0 9 8 6 9 0 3 1 2 0 *